YOU ARE

THE

CREATOR

RIANA ARENDSE

ISBN: 0620862890

?

Cover Design: Debbie Boettcher

Interior Design: Bilal Idrees

Editor: Mark Johnston

The Author of this book does not dispense medical advice or prescribe the use of any technique as a form of treatment for physical, emotional, or medical problems without the advice of a physician, either directly or indirectly. The intent of the author is only to offer information of a general nature to help you in your quest for emotional and spiritual well-being. In the event you use any of the information in this book for yourself, the author and the publisher assume no responsibility for your actions.

CONTENTS

Acknowledgements

First and Always I want to acknowledge the Source, the Divine of everything that is in this book and that writes through me, allowing this book to come into creation. I would like to thank the following people for their support: Henk Erasmus my partner, my love, a man of great wisdom and compassion; without his support this book would not have been possible. My beautiful boy Rihon Iza, whose mere presence encouraged me to continue with my purpose work and new creations of love. My parents Charles and Agnes for being the catalyst for my entire journey and for all they have given to me. My brother Bradley and his wife Carlene for their love and support – I appreciate you. My parents in law Annette and Gerhard my gratitude is deep and abiding.

To those who have inspired me and were teachers, students and mirrors along the way, I thank you. Thanks to everyone who has attended my workshops, master classes, and pursued my healing modalities, teachings and my work. Your support for my efforts means more to me than I can express. This book is dedicated also to all of you who, in your desire for enlightenment, awakening and well-being, have asked the questions and are ready to begin to remember and integrate the teachings in this book.

"When we surrender, we can experience our darkest moment as our greatest catalyst for transformation and expansion. Suffering will then cease, and a movement will be catalyzed."

-Riana Arendse-

Introduction

"Know this book is for you... your journey, your awakening, your healing, your remembering, your Un-becoming...your potential and yourself"

Imagine being a dolphin, thrown into a bowl with goldfish, and told to... deal with it!

Well that is how I would describe the feeling that imprisoned me - ever since I incarnated into this life. I finally heard those resonating and liberating words after many years of struggling to understand my lifelong pain. I rejoiced when I heard them because they gave meaning to my fractured life, shed light on the dark sense of imprisonment that defined me, and ultimately unlocked the door to My Spiritual Awakening.

Hearing those words for the first time resonated with me deeply because they described the exact way I felt inside but could never fully understand or explain. Those simple words helped me 'see' myself for what I really was—a prisoner—and made me long to be free.

Most importantly, they unlocked the door to my spiritual awakening.

My wakeup call, spiritual awakening, remembering; had been a repetitive incessant cycle of suffering and unwinding dissolution ... until I finally realized I had been endlessly striving in vain to become something beyond my grasp: HAPPY.

For all of us in fact, the spiritual awakening journey can be quite disastrous, eye opening but a necessary gift, nonetheless. This is a brief story of my Journey Home, my journey of Un-becoming, and the soul's persistent call to realizing ones innate and true power. The journey of realizing who this is that has inhabited these bodies .... time and time again, life after life.

I use the word Un-becoming a lot in this book. In short, it refers to the process of unlearning everything you've ever learned so you can ascend to a higher and deeper level of spiritual understanding.

You? Yes you, the person reading this book now.

Know that this book is for you.

While I have chronicled my spiritual journey, I've only done so to help you find yours. Your awakening, your healing, and your remembering. Your Un-becoming, your potential, and yourself.

As you truly are.

The mere fact that you were led to pick up this book and read it is an unconscious calling to you, perhaps to activate your spiritual awakening; to catalyze your healing and Un-becoming, or to realize who and what you really are.

It is the quest for knowledge and understanding about yourself that moved you to read this book. It is the same quest that moved me to write it.

Un-becoming

Embarking on a spiritual journey—the process of healing—will not require you to become anything; rather, it will require you Un-become everything you ever thought you were, everything you thought you had to be, all your beliefs, conditions, behaviors, and thoughts.

Through the process of Un-becoming, everything you know will be removed.

The purpose of Un-becoming is to find, discover, and remember who you truly are beneath the masks, the personas, the illusion. Hence all the complex layers of your personas and personal story's will be shed, including everything you've accumulated to form you, so at last your soul can rest in the bare, naked truth of who you are.

The Origin Of This Book

This is something I have been putting off for quite some time. Not out of Fear or judgement, but as a necessary part of my journey; I have waited for the time when I intuitively feel inspired and called to share my journey of Un-becoming, healing and self-mastery...

I would briefly like to tell you my story and how I came to be a Healer and Spiritual Teacher...and how this book came to be in existence. I would not ask you to go on this journey with me with an open mind, heart and soul and lift above that which is your mind, if I did not first open my heart to you and share with you the story of how I got to where I am today.

I know there are many authors out there who write spiritual knowledge books to help people discover their true identity and inherent power. However, I've found there aren't many books that teach people how to apply knowledge gleaned from spiritual awakening to one's physical reality—especially regarding the healing process and learning to live as one's true, divine self.

This book is designed to disrupt the way you see the world, specifically your inner world, and share valuable tools to help you shift your world, through subconscious and conscious changes, within your being. As you read the content, I'm confident you will begin to experience spiritual awakening. Why? Because once you begin "seeing" the patterns I unveil, you will not be able to "unsee" them. Being Present and being spiritually conscious as a daily practice, is an integral part of living in truth, however it tends to be difficult at times to hold this space and truth when one is continuously triggered by one's pain and conditioned ways of being, behavior and beliefs. This process is necessary because of the years of untruth, conditioned beliefs, trauma and habitual patterns all of us has come to endure and live. And so, I write this book as a step by step guide and course on how to begin to heal and master the self so as to move from suffering into Love, and from the small self into the higher self or God Self. These are the exact tools and daily practices I have used to heal and master myself and still live this each and every day.

In that spirit, the first part of this book focuses on my journey of Un-becoming, healing, and self-mastery, how I came to be a healer and spiritual teacher, and how this book came to be.

In the second part of the book, we will journey through awakening, remembering, and the transformative steps of Un-becoming, healing, and self-mastery. All these steps will among other things, help you learn to be present as a daily practice, which is an essential part of living in truth. If you are eager and willing to change, the actionable knowledge I will share has the power to shift and uplift your mind on a vibrational, subconscious and emotional level.

Though the knowledge and insights I've shared in this book have been gleaned from my healing journey, they are rooted in the transmissions from the Divine, as well as the ascended masters with whom I work. The words in this book have been energetically attuned to initiate healing, awakenings and, for others, even massive shifts in perspective. The basis of this book is what I have learned and mastered along my healing journey. With the help from the collective ascended masters, archangels and my higher self, I'm pleased to present you with this step-by-step guide to Un-becoming all that you are and have come to be. With channelled texts from the Divine, as well as energetic attunements that will raise your vibrational frequency to a higher octave, as well as a step-by-step approach to mastering oneself.

It not only the very process I have mastered to heal myself and truly step into the truth of my soul, but also a modality you can use to heal yourself instantly, which has proven valuable to my myself, my clients, and my students. The healing process is one of Un-becoming all that you were, all that you thought you had to be, and a complete surrender of the small self. When understood, practiced, and mastered, these concepts will help you create the life you yearn for.

The essence of the teachings in this book, will be found within yourself and not within the words. It is good to remember to feel as you read, as the words are no more than signposts, and to which they point is to a must deeper dimension within yourself. A true spiritual teacher does not have anything to give or to add to you, rather a true spiritual teacher's role is to help remove that which separates you from the truth of who you already are and what you already know in the deepest parts of your being. The writings within this book are sacred and come out of a state of experiential and conceptual consciousness, of which we may call Source. The teachings in this book does not belong to any one religion or spiritual tradition, but are immediately accessible to all of humanity. Inherent in this, is that there is a sense of urgency here. The transformation of humanity's consciousness is no longer n gift, so to speak, only available to a select few individuals, but a necessity if humankind is to awaken out of the calamities in which it finds itself. It is these remembrances that will save and transform the world as it were.

Ultimately, it is my sincere hope this book helps you begin to heal and master yourself so you can make the beautiful leap from suffering to Love, and from the small self to the higher self or God Self.

I will also tell you this:

No one who reads this book will be left unchanged or at least a part of them will Un-become.

CHAPTER 1:

In The Beginning

Sometimes life must really suck for you to want to end it... and
wake up

I entered this reality, this incarnation, as a severely empathic child. Ever since I can remember, I've always felt out of place—like I didn't belong—and I could never understand why. This dolphin-out-of-water phenomena became evident in my family relationship dynamics and, not long after that, in my external reality, social circles, and later in my intimate relationships.

Unbeknownst to them, neither of my parents had healed from their own emotional trauma, subconscious beliefs, and conditioning before I was born. Still, they strived to do all they could to provide a good upbringing for my brother and me. I cherish many wonderful moments and memories with my family; but in comparison to what followed, they barely made a dent in the childhood I truly desired.

I don't share the pain of my own upbringing and familial relationships to draw attention to myself, but rather to reveal how children can be scarred, limited, and affected on a very deep level from wounds other than those caused by overt physical, sexual, or verbal abuse. Unbeknownst to many people, these non-physical wounds can lead to deep loneliness and other issues that—if left unresolved—can last a lifetime. When people's lives turn into a downward spiral of negative experiences and relationships, the root of their pain can often be traced back to their childhood experiences and upbringing.

Unsafety

Having incarnated into this reality we call "life" as a severely empathic being, I could sense things in people—their emotions, traumas, and hurts—and feel them deep in my being as if they were my own. I didn't know my empathic capabilities were actually extrasensory gifts with names (clairsentience, meaning clear feeling; claircognizance, meaning clear knowing; and clairaudience, meaning clear hearing) until later. All I knew was that somehow I knew things about situations and people, could feel spiritual presence, and could receive messages through dreams, even prophetic dreams.

For the most part, I didn't think I was special in any way. I was mostly quiet, shy, and lacked self-esteem and confidence. In other words, I didn't feel like a "special little girl."

While I excelled at school and in singing and music, I never really understood the point of it all. All I knew was that I needed to excel and prove I was an achiever. Why? Because I needed validation and acknowledgement and... love.

Like the dolphin in the fish bowl, I felt so out of place.

Unbeknownst to anyone, including my parents, I experienced pain, inner conflict, and confusion early on.

The pain, inner conflict and confusion that had begun so early on in my psyche, my being, had already taken a toll on me, and no one knew. Soon I began sensing that something—maybe everything—was not right in my life or the world.

It's like I was born with a Spiritual Immune System, Spiritual Inner Mechanism that did not align with nor agree with the illusory worldview, imposed upon me through Social Conditioning and limiting beliefs due to my upbringing. I began sensing that much was not right in my life as well as within the world and started asking questions internally. This was a concurrent inner anomaly that plagued me since the day I was born, I just could not pinpoint it until my early adult life. This was the inner conflict I had been living with since my arrival.

But while endless storms of capricious conflict raged inside me, one question persisted from childhood to adulthood: Is this really all there is? That is, am I just here to be miserable, conform to what the world says I should be, and suffer? Is life limited to attaining things and conforming to the rules of the world?

My father, being an alcoholic, was a source of great anxiety throughout my childhood because I never knew what to expect from day to day. His intention was never to harm or scar me—he was an amazing man in many ways—however, I knew he was dealing with his own unhealed wounds. Addictions are 'coping' or 'saving' modalities used to alleviate specific pains in people's lives. Specific pains cause people to gravitate towards specific addictions. The pain that fuels alcoholism comes from emotional insecurity—feeling emotionally unsafe in relation to others. I call this "unsafety."

Unsafety leads to social anxiety, which is a hallmark of alcoholism (though many alcoholics don't recognize or admit it). Unsafety often originates from trauma experienced in a dysfunctional home. In my experience, it's not possible to develop alcoholism unless you come from a background of dysfunctional relationships, beginning with the people you were exposed to during childhood.

In my practice and personal experience, I've found few people are consciously aware they have been traumatized, or that there is an underlying reason to explain why they are the way they are. Instead, most people just think their addiction is a character defect, a predisposition to addiction, or due to stress. For example, my father ascribed his addiction to the stressors of his relationship with my mother, his financial situation, or his job. People often don't see the dysfunction in their current relationships is a mirror of the dysfunction in their childhood relationships. Though it is often easier for people to recognize the dysfunction in their current relationships than it is to realize that the current dysfunction is a mirror reflection of the dysfunction of their childhood relationships.

The pain that unites alcoholics is the feeling that relationships are not safe, especially emotionally. If you never know who to trust and you're always on high alert, waiting to be blamed or attacked by someone, you feel unsafe in relationship to people. Ultimately, addiction provides an outwardly, comfortable, pseudo-reality for emotionally traumatized people. At the same time, it insulates them from having to confront painful, up-welling emotions, which they believe would be too painful to process and cope with.

In essence, keeping trauma as unconscious as possible is the ultimate utility of addiction.

Alcoholics often mistakenly believe their drinking is not affecting anyone. Of course, that's not true; the children of alcoholics are often the most impacted. The truth is, the effects of growing up around alcoholism are sometimes so profound that they last a lifetime, affecting the way the child-turned-adult sees themselves and others, interacts in relationships, and more.

Children of one or more alcoholic parents may find themselves thinking they are different from others and therefore not good enough. Some find it difficult to give themselves a break, compare themselves to others, and feel they aren't good enough. This results in low self-worth, low self-esteem, and deep feelings of inadequacy.

I speak not only as a professional healer, but from first-hand experience. As a child, and even up until adulthood, I always sought approval from my father. I never felt and believed I was enough. I always thought I needed to do more and be more. Why? Because I never heard "I love you." Because I never had the true, emotional connection I so longed for and needed with either of my parents. Hence though my childhood had many happy moments, and I have many fond memories, I always felt an inner conflict between what I was experiencing in the outside world and what I was feeling inside.

Without a good example to follow from their childhood, children of alcoholics never experience traditional or harmonious family relationships and are left to figure out what it means to be normal. Because alcohol use is normalized in families with alcoholism, children often struggle to distinguish between good and bad role models. Hence many end up feeling conflicted, confused, and self-conscious when they realize that drinking is not considered normal in other families.

After growing up in an atmosphere where denial, lying, and keeping secrets may have been the norm, children can develop serious trust problems. Broken promises of the past make them think trusting someone will end up backfiring on them in the future. As a result of trust issues or lack of self-esteem, they often struggle with romantic relationships and avoid getting close to others. Consequently, they avoid social situations, have difficulty making friends, and isolate themselves.

If an alcoholic parent was mean or abusive, the affected child can grow up with an irrational fear of all anger and angry people. Thus, many spend their lives avoiding conflict or confrontation of any kind out of fear the conflict will turn violent or lead to a bad outcome of some sort. For that reason, they often associate social events with trauma, tension, or feelings of dread and either have difficulty lightening up at them or avoid them altogether.

Some adult children of alcoholics find it difficult to give themselves a break, which is why many engage in severe self-critique, which leads to anxiety, depression, and social isolation. In addition to judging themselves too harshly, many constantly seek approval from others and become people-pleasers who get easily-crushed when someone is not happy with them and live in fear of any kind of criticism.

To avoid criticism, or the anger of their alcoholic parent, many children and adults from alcoholic homes become super responsible perfectionists, overachievers, and/or workaholics. On the other hand, it is common for a person to go the opposite direction and mirror the same bad behaviors they witnessed during childhood. If an alcoholic parent was emotionally or physically unavailable, the adult child can develop a debilitating fear of abandonment and, as a result, cling to toxic relationships simply because they don't want to be alone. Children of alcoholics endure chronic and extreme levels of tension and stress in myriad ways.

Due to being on the receiving end of alcoholism, my mom—unbeknownst to her—was also suffering from deep wounds of low self-worth and low self-love. It is no coincidence my dad was essentially a mirror of her own alcoholic father. The effect on me? Aside from occasional surface-level joy and happiness, my home environment was rife with anxiety, deep emotional scarcity, shallow emotional connections, and instability.

It wasn't easy seeing my mother and father suffer so deeply, and I always felt the need to save them. But I couldn't at the time. Unbeknownst to me, this was the life and experiences I had chosen for myself prior to my incarnation into this life and thus necessary triggers and guideposts for my spiritual expansion. To be sure, those mirrors and experiences enabled me to finally awaken to my divine power and walk my purpose. My parents were mere divine souls who agreed to play out these experiences with me to assist me in discovering my path. And so, I was too a mirror for them to find their inner light. Everyone's journey is different and when we incarnate into this life, everyone in your life plays a part which serves your expansion. There

14

are no victims and perpetrators, just a spiritual journey unfolding. There are no negatives or positives, everything just points you back to love and back to truth. The parent and child relationship were always meant to be a partnership in expansion and awakening. Period.

At any rate, I've learned why it is so hard for people to socially integrate, function, connect, and unite. It's because we are emotionally separated. Emotional separation, and the profound loneliness that comes from it, is the cause of all unhappiness in humanity. It is the root cause of addictions, of suicide, of acts of terror, and the dysfunctional structure of society. We, as a society, have lost our motive and thus ability to perceive and connect with one another at an emotional level. And emotional unsafety is at the heart of the problem.

Conditioned Beliefs

For most of us, beliefs about God, religion, the world, money, success, love, and everything else are conditioned into us from a very early age. In my case, I was conditioned to believe: Life is hard, the rich get richer and the poor get poorer, and success meant having money and nice things. Therefore, to be financially successful, I needed to work extremely hard and make many sacrifices—even if it meant being in a career field or job that sacrificed my own inner happiness. I was brought up in a religious family where I was taught that our specific church was the right way and that we were the chosen ones.

Sound familiar?

Based on the example that my parent's marriage displayed, I was shown what love looks like. And that became my subconscious definition of love...and yet my inner guidance system would be conflicted because I knew true unconditional love was not supposed to look this way. The relationships we choose later on in life are often very similar to our parent's relationship. The type of relationship your parents had, whether their relationship was long term, whether they got divorced, whether positive or negative can affect your choice of relationships in adulthood and in addition will allow you to subconsciously attract similar types of relationships into your life. In essence, your parental relationships provide you with a subconscious relationship blueprint for the future.

I was also conditioned to believe I must conform to society and not follow my inner guidance system, especially if my inner guidance system directed me to do something or be someone that was socially unacceptable. Unintentionally I was conditioned to believe that I must endlessly strive to have more and be more. These conditioned beliefs conflicted with what I felt in my heart. And yet I conformed and took those burdens on to please my parents and make them proud.

All that said, I'm so thankful for the roles my parents played on my journey, even though the beliefs they instilled in me were misguided. I've learned my parents were mere divine souls who agreed to play out these experiences with me to aid me in discovering my path so I could serve as a mirror for them to find their own inner lights.

While everyone's journey is different, when you incarnate into this life everyone you encounter plays a part in your expansion. There are no victims and perpetrators, just an unfolding spiritual journey. There are no negatives or positives; everything points back to love and truth. The parent-child relationship was always meant to be a partnership in expansion and awakening. Period.

I share my own testimony here to show how each of us hold beliefs, values, thoughts, assumptions, and motivations that we have never questioned or examined.

When I finally recognized the trauma and limiting beliefs in my own life had been carried down from generation to generation, I knew I was the one who would eventually put an end to the cycle. The buck needed to stop with me.

As my healing journey began, I questioned every single one of my conditioned beliefs. As I downloaded knowledge from the divine, I came to gradually realize my reality was the creation of my own beliefs. When my beliefs shifted, my reality shifted with them. That is when I realized I was, as the book title states, the CREATOR of my own reality.

In subsequent sections, I share my childhood journey to truth, as well as some questions and signposts to help you find yours.

We must consider that we hold beliefs, values, thoughts, assumptions and motivations that we have never questioned or examined. We inherited them and pass them on, regardless of whether they are chains that imprison us or keys that set us free.

Suppressed Emotions

Other than conditioned beliefs mentioned in the previous part, there is one other thing that deems quite detrimental to children growing up, and immensely limits their ability to function at their highest potential in later years. And these are unprocessed emotions. When natural emotions go unprocessed, it usually results in it becoming suppressed.

As a matter of fact, the mental health of society is far from ideal. Rates of stress, depression, and anxiety are increasing. There are likely many reasons for this, including a rapidly changing society, higher levels of loneliness and isolation, misguided attempts to medicate negative feelings, and existential confusion about the truths of who we really are as spiritual beings. But perhaps the most important reason I see, is that people seem deeply confused about the nature of emotions and how to process them.

Adults also have an explicit public self-consciousness system. That is, they know that other people can see their emotional reactions if they act on them and they must then consider how others will respond to their emotions. It is because of these different streams of consciousness that emotional processing can become very conflicted in humans in general. And this conflict results in parts or aspects of oneself in becoming fractured or dissociated.

Consider the following example. Luke is age 6 and learning how to ride his bike. He falls and scrapes his knee and runs over to his father, crying. Think about the impact of his father's response if he says, "Stop crying. Boys don't cry. Don't be a girl!" As opposed to, "I am so sorry you are hurt! Let me give you a hug." The different responses mean very different things for how such feelings will be expressed in the future. And, as Luke grows into an adolescent, it will have strong implications for how he privately judges his own feelings.

Such an unprocessed state does not just disappear into the ether. Instead, it is stored deep into one's subconscious mind. It becomes suppressed.

As a child, when you were excited what did you do? Jump around and clap your hands or maybe even laugh or scream?

How about when you were upset, did you throw a tantrum or become frustrated?

Wasn't it so easy to feel, express and resolve your emotions then? Until of course, someone told you to stop it and that it was wrong or unacceptable, and you learned not to show your emotions. If you vomited would you swallow back your vomit? And yet as adults, we are sometimes conditioned not to show or even feel our emotions.

While it is correct that throwing a tantrum in the office would not be accepted or even be considered an ideal working situation, yet it is important to have a means of letting out and processing emotions in a safe way.

Not just the negative emotions like anger and sadness. Even, the uplifting emotions like joy and excitement.

I remember as a child being taught not to be angry as anger is unacceptable. As a result, I did not express this for over 28 years and bottled everything up.

Anger is just an expression of an emotion. It is not good or bad. It is just a natural expression. It is a process of letting a natural emotion out, releasing it and processing it. But In my case, I was told that my feelings or emotions were not valid or acceptable and so I suppressed it for most of my life.

Fear was also a huge thing for me, I lived in a constant state of fear and panic all my life. Not only because of the experiences I had as a child, but I was taught that the having of the fear was ridiculous. If I had a sudden fear of a spider, I was laughed at and made to feel like the fear I was experiencing wasn't warranted. And so, I suppressed my fear and bottled every fearful encounter I had. And from my early childhood to adulthood I had lived in a state of chronic fear and panic. And then in my later years I began attracting men into my life who were angry or men who would make me fearful. They were merely mirroring to me the part of myself that I suppressed. We will go more into this in the next part when we discuss the Law of Attraction.

Now let's consider what happens if someone is trying to block these emotions all the time. More and more mental energy will be squeezed into the subconscious mind. Moreover, the self-consciousness system will very likely use increasingly harsh and critical language to inhibit the feelings— "Stop feeling this way!" "What is wrong with you!?" "This is pointless, stop being so stupid". Not only do these elements inhibit the original feeling, but they also generate core feelings in and of themselves. That is, the core feeling self will feel wounded and judged by the self-consciousness system, which creates a bad intrapsychic cycle, a cycle where an individual turn against themselves, which can easily lead to depression. Unprocessed emotion (dense energy) also then doesn't just leave the body, it stores itself within our body, specifically our organs. Which later then becomes physical manifestations such as physical illnesses.

There are 5 main emotions, which consist of grief, anger, envy, fear, and love. And within these, there are also the highest intention level which is Love or Fear.

Ultimately, all thoughts are underwritten by love or fear. This is the great polarity. Everything, ultimately, comes down to one of these, in the simplest form. All judgments, ideas, perceptions, understandings, decisions, and actions are based in one of these. However ultimately, there is only one.

Love.

Even fear is an extension of love, and when used effectively, expresses love.

The difficulty comes in when any of the five natural emotions become suppressed or distorted. Then they become incongruous, and not identifiable at all as extensions of love. Specifically, unidentifiable from our caregivers or parents' perspectives, as they too were taught and raised the same way.

20

Grief is a pure emotion. Grief that is constantly suppressed becomes chronic depression.

Anger is a pure emotion. Anger that is constantly suppressed becomes rage and eventually anguish, a very abnormal emotion.

Envy is a pure emotion. Envy that is constantly suppressed becomes jealousy, a very abnormal emotion.

Fear is a pure emotion. The purpose of fear is to develop a bit of vigilance or caution. Caution is a tool that helps keep one alive. It is an extension of Self-love.

Fear continually suppressed becomes panic, a very unnatural emotion.

Love is a natural emotion. Love that is continually suppressed becomes possessiveness, a very unnatural emotion.

And so, it is that these pure emotions, when suppressed, produce abnormal reactions, responses and behaviors later on in our adulthood

In these cases, what needs to happen is, that we need to reintegrate those suppressed parts back into wholeness and we need to give approval to those emotions, by giving our inner child what he/she so needed but did not get. This we will dive more into at a later stage during the Un-becoming Process.

The Mirror of my Subconscious began reflecting in my reality

Allow me to explain what I mean by "the mirror of my subconscious began reflecting in my reality".

The consciousness we call Source/God/the Universe created the law of attraction/mirroring, as a learning matrix or holographic illusion so to speak, that would facilitate expansion and growth, which gives us the ability to attract things, people, situations and places into our reality that we are a vibrational match to. It accomplishes this through the law of attraction in that everything that is within you vibrationally is reflected externally in your external world.

You can only experience things that are a vibrational match to you. For example, a person who has low self-esteem, attracts circumstances, people, places, and events etc. that are a match to the vibration of low self-esteem. But the reason I mention the mirror of my subconscious, is because 95% of what we actually attract into our lives are subconscious beliefs, programs and traumas that we are not consciously aware of. We are not aware of these hidden beliefs that seem to run our lives. To the subconscious mind time doesn't exist so even if it was an early childhood belief or event or unprocessed trauma it makes no difference to the subconscious mind. Past issues are not actually in the past. In the metaphysical world and in the subconscious mind, beyond what we can see, time doesn't really exist; that is, everything is actually happening in the now, the present. This means the negative of energy of a past trauma, program, or belief is still lingering within your "field." Your field is you, your physical and metaphysical presence. Now that you know what I mean by "mirror of the subconscious," I think my childhood story I wrote about in the introduction will make a lot more sense.

I was only a child, but I felt as if I didn't belong – that I didn't really fit in anywhere. But that lonely feeling and isolation was nothing compared to what came next.

In an instant I lost my entire childhood, and lost it over and over and over again, and all events that followed; mirrored this with increasing intensity.

I cannot remember the exact age, as most of my childhood and adolescence was blocked out due to the trauma experienced. Something that most children do during traumatic experiences is to disassociate from one's body, to escape the traumatic experience.

But nevertheless, this part was where my life as I knew it, had come to an end, and the external mirror of my hidden subconscious wounding, would become evident in my reality.

I was roughly between the ages of 5 and 8 when it happened. It took my innocence from me. It was the event that caused me to believe no one could be trusted, no one was there for me, and that I was all alone in this world. And it happened at the hands of people I knew and didn't know, who should have been protecting and loving me.

When I say "it," I am referring to the first time—of many times—I was raped.

It was then that I knew that there was no one I could trust and no one I could escape to. I was all alone in this world.

What had happened to me at the hands of people I knew and didn't know who should be protecting and loving me, was a painful knowing.

The mirror of my subconscious wounding began reflecting with more intensity as the years went by....

After the first time I was raped, many other people sexually abused me too—albeit with "love."

I say Love, two-fold; because looking back now, based on what I know now, I see they too are also victims of victims. An incessant cycle of suffering and abuse, from one generation to the next; and so, the manner in which I was groomed by some of them, was done with ease and calmness.

I was very mature for my age, but a frightened little girl nonetheless. I was already introverted and shy; but the abuse started, I retreated even deeper into my shell and became even more timid.

I honestly cannot even recall the countless number of times and number of people who took my childhood from me over and over again. I felt like I had a sign on my forehead that said, "Take me, use me, hurt me."

As the years of sexual abuse and trauma passed, my inner conflict escalated. I was lost, miserable, moody, and thought maybe my hopelessly tormented life was the one I was meant to have. I tried to accept it was simply my fate.

What do you remember from your childhood?

Do you remember having moments of being aware that something was changing for you, that the adults around you were inauthentic at times?

For many, it can be earlier, it just depends on how early conditioning takes hold.

The Reflection in the Mirror grew Larger

By the age of 15, I was defiant and acting out. I became rebellious, drank alcohol, and occasionally did drugs. My parents were very worried and distressed about my chronic unhappiness. They saw most of the red flags but misinterpreted them as me being youthfully disobedient.

One night, I went with a friend from school to her boyfriend's place, some sort of house party I suppose. Just the two of us girls with a bunch of guys. I don't even recall drinking that night. As everyone was leaving, I was standing outside the house, and my friend was in the house with her boyfriend. One of the guys was staring at me from his car. The next thing I knew, he was standing in front of me. He was older than me, in his late twenties.

He grabbed me, lifted me up and put me in his car.

I froze.

I knew what was coming but also, I wasn't sure. In that instant, I had frozen within myself, my mind and my body. The level of fear that overcame me was paralyzing. One would think after all I had endured, that I should be used to it by now.... right?

I felt panicky but without a sense of direction, felt hopeless and trapped. I remember having a strong desire to get out of the situation, but I didn't know how. I felt that any action I might take, might make the situation worse.

If you've ever been startled and your body started running before you ever thought "oh no, I should get out of here" that was your flight mechanism at work. Fight and flight are both active defences in that they are ways to stop something bad from happening. However, freeze is different. The brain uses freeze when there is no perceived way out. It's used as a method to try to reduce the likelihood or intensity of harm. Like a deer in headlights, you tend to freeze when you are not sure what to do to escape danger.

Unfortunately, painfully, freeze is read by many as consent. But it isn't.

Freeze is much more likely if you have experienced trauma before. It is the body screaming for safety in the only way it knows how. It is the senses being overwhelmed to the point of immobility. It is terror masked as detachment or numbness ....and I was terrified.

He then proceeded to speed off without saying a word, and takes me to an abandoned forest like area, with no one insight, maybe about 20 minutes away from where my friend was. The feeling I had gotten from him seemed dark, and I was too afraid to even say a word at this point. Many thoughts rushed through my head: maybe he just wants to talk... or kill me... or rape me... again.

Driving down a gravel roadway deeper into the forest, the night sky and surroundings grew darker and darker. Until he eventually stops the car and parks.

He eventually stopped and ordered me to take off my clothes. When I refused, he smashed my head into the passenger window. He had hit me across the head with his gun.

He opened his trousers, grabbed my head and hands, and forced me to perform oral sex on him. It happened so shockingly fast that I didn't have a chance to resist. I wouldn't have been able to overcome his strength anyway. I was terrified but sort of emotionless at the same time.

I was also horrified by the sight, the smell, and the enormity of him in my mouth. I was gagging and heaving, and tears were running down my face. It went on for what felt like hours. When he climaxed in my mouth, and all over my face and chest, I was sick.

Then he suddenly acted normal again, as if nothing happened. I had thought it to be over, but it soon dawned on me that the ordeal had just begun.

After a few minutes he said, "Take your clothes off."

When I refused again, he pointed the gun at my head, repeated himself, and ordered me to sit on top of him. I tried to hover over him, but he suddenly forced me to sit all the way down. The penetrating pain was horrific as I struggled to lift myself off him.

With tears streaming down my face, I felt like I was being ripped apart. Terrible, searing, hot pain spread from between my legs to my stomach. My whole body convulsed in pain.

When he was done, I sat back in my seat and put my hand between my legs to compress the pain. After sobbing uncontrollably for a few minutes, I removed my hand from my legs and was horrified to see it was covered in blood.

At that moment, I asked him to please take me home. He replied, "No, you will die tonight." I don't know what came over me, but suddenly I decided I would rather die than be raped again. I opened the car door and walked. "Come back here!" he said in a harsh voice. I said, "No, if you're going to shoot me, then shoot me, but I'm going!"

He drove off. I walked out of the dark forest and eventually found my way to the main highway, which was not far from home.

When I returned home, I softly slipped into the bathroom. Looking at my face in the mirror, I had never seen such sorrow in my eyes. When I saw the greyish substance caked all over my face and chest, I fell to the bathroom floor and burst into tears. I didn't know why I had to be so cursed. I cried from my soul:

Why can't be happy like other kids? Why did God put me here on this earth to live this horrible life?

My parents didn't know a thing about all the sexual assault I had endured, and I wasn't going to tell them. I was too ashamed and didn't think they would understand. I didn't know if it was even safe to tell.

So, I had been holding all these secrets for years and nobody knew. I was living in a dark hole and wanted to die. Death was my constant thought, as I didn't see any other way out my depression and misery. I hated myself. I got so used to being sad that sadness itself became my friend. I had no idea how to love myself.

This was my reality.

And this would mirror my unconsciousness with even more intensity as the years went by.

The Recurring Theme and Pattern – My Core Wound

As a teenager, I experimented with alcohol and smoking. At the time, I thought I was just having fun. But looking back, I was just trying to escape my painful reality. I felt trapped most of my life, and the stimulants offered temporary freedom from pain.

Not long after I was raped, I went with some friends to another friend's house to have some fun and escape reality for a little while. The house was cold, and I was only wearing a short skirt and sleeveless top, so the owner of the house—a big, burly guy in his thirties or forties—said I was welcome to get a jacket from the other room. When I walked to the room, which was just outside the front door of the house, he followed me. As soon as I stepped in the room, he grabbed me from behind, around my neck. Suddenly my cheek was wet with the smell of brandy and Coke. The scent itself made my insides clench and my throat close in terror. I tried to fight. But I was overpowered. He pushed me into the dark room and violated me. Fixing my eyes on a picture on the wall, I couldn't believe I was being savagely attacked with my friends in the next room. He lifted his body from mine, swore, and kicked me. I stopped moving. I stopped screaming into his hand, which was firmly clamped over my mouth. I would be staring at the purple shadows his fingertips left on my cheeks a week later.

My breath came in fragmented, faltering shakes. When he bore down on me, his weight and movement burned the rough carpet against my skin. The sudden invasion tore me from my body. Then the pain pulled me back in. The violence turned my body into a flopping fish, struggling against the air. It felt like my cheekbone exploded under the first slap. The second, third, fourth made my face numb.

When he was done, he got up, got dressed, and said, "This is your own fault, you asked for it, wearing that short skirt! And you will say nothing to no one!"

I laid there in fear, for what felt like an eternity, before picking myself up. I tried to repair the elastic on my skirt and remember why I was there. Then I went back to the main area where my friends were. I could see the looks on their faces; it was fear.

They knew.

They were too scared to confront him or call the police. As they walked me home, no one really talked about what just happened. I felt so alone.

I berated myself all the way home and back into the darkness of my room again. Maybe, I thought, if I could fix this one thing, dress differently, it would be as though it never happened. I blamed myself even though it wasn't my fault. In denial, I shoved it as far back in my mind as I could, trying to dismiss it as a bad decision—until the avalanche of pain buried me even further into depression, shame, and self-blame.

At night, I huddled under my comforter and wished I could die. Too scared to tell my parents what had been happening all my life, I learned to silently cry into my pillow. During the daytime I tried to keep it together. But at night, all my pain floated to the surface. It took me hours to fall asleep, and the nightmares kicked me awake. I had assumed rape was a physical injury. I thought that once the bruises on my thighs and arms faded, I would be healed. I didn't account for the hollowing out of my mind, dissociating from my energetic body and my fragmented sense of self.

For all my life, I kept silent about my rapes. It was a shameful secret lodged in my throat, ready to choke me every time I contemplated telling. I was afraid of how my loved ones would react—that they'd confirm it was my fault or refuse to believe it happened in the first place. There was a time I remember when I actually tried to count in my mind the number of separate times, I had been sexually assaulted, and I stopped counting, because the number seemed endless. My fear, shame and my rapist's threats created this silence, but I was the one who kept feeding it. Eventually, my secrets became as destructive as the rapes itself. I thought my parents would be ashamed of me if I told. I believed it when my rapist called me a slut, blamed myself and was sure everyone else would, too.

If one cannot run from inevitable harm and one cannot fight inevitable harm, and one expects inevitable harm; one will instead freeze and dissociate from their body. It is a practice that becomes an art form for those of us who lived at the mercy of abuse. We become fragmented individuals who live in various states of dissociation from the physical world and most especially our physical bodies, which was the only way to survive our lives, our situations, our realities. I have dissociated from my body to prevent feeling past pain and to avoid feeling future pain. (After all, if you don't deserve it, why is the abuse happening to you?)

I also did not care how other people used my body. If a woman gets raped, she feels like she is dirty, damaged, violated. She feels as if something of herself has been taken from her. Rape can alter the course of a woman's entire life. This happens because she identifies with her body. She is attached to her body. So, what happens if you are raped over and over and over again? You have 2 choices. Either you can't survive it, so you let your body die. Or you stop caring what happens to your body. You detach from it and you stop seeing it as yourself. I no longer cared who used my body or how they used it.

From my early adulthood, I begun to suffer the physical illnesses related to these emotional traumas. I had suffered autoimmune illnesses, depression, panic attacks, anxiety, paralyzing fear, polycystic ovarian syndrome, loss of weight, rheumatoid arthritis and the list goes on. The vibration and frequency or metaphysical cause for autoimmune disorders and the like; is always unfathomable and deep-seated self-hate. I could feel the imbalances in my body. I could hear my skin, my organs, my bones, my blood, my womb, as if they were yelling to me "please help!".

By my early twenties, I had been through a harrowing journey of pain, suffering, turmoil, and numerous rapes and abuse. I was damaged. I was a dead person walking. And while I made many plans to end my life, I had no idea why I could never find the courage to take the final step.

To be sure, even though I could see no end in sight, no light in the darkness, there was always an inner sense of hope that I could NOT shake. No matter how much I just wanted to give up, some unseen force inside my being wouldn't allow me to quit.

Until my 30th year of life, I lived in a state of almost continuous anxiety, including social anxiety, interspersed with periods of suicidal depression. As I write this, it feels like I am talking about some past lifetime or someone else's life.

Most of us were not taught as children how to meet experiences by being present with them and processing them, without turning away or disassociating. Instead we store these unprocessed memories in our body/subconscious minds for later in life, in need of love, attention and resolution.

What is your Core Wound?

All that matters is YOUR perception, your journey, your path to Self-Realisation. All your power is within you, not on the outside. The dream (this life in the sleep state) holds and presents the clues. And so perfectly designed for YOU, by YOU.

To understand and believe your power to create your own reality, you must first understand two big things about your soul's journey. First, it is my firm belief and experience that our souls are eternal and thus exist long before our physical bodies come into this world. And before each of us are born, we choose the main goal or theme we want to experience in this reality. This becomes our soul's purpose. In my case, I've learned my soul chose to experience true liberation/freedom in this life so I could realize the powerful being that I am.

Second, and this is the hard part, in order for us to experience and achieve our soul's true purpose, we must experience the opposite of it. I call this opposite our "core wound." For example, in order to know love, we must know hate. Experiencing and feeling our core wound places us in a negative state. That negative state impels us to desire (and seek) our soul's true desire, the positive state. My core wound was the opposite of freedom and power: imprisonment of my mind and powerlessness.

Before we are born into this life, this reality, we have already decided what the main desire or theme is that we would like to experience. And these intentions basically set the tone for all the situations we will have experienced for the duration of our lives here.

This goal or life experience we intend for ourselves includes choosing our parents, for their specific roles they would play in us reaching this experience or goal. I will use my life for example, I opted into this life to experience true liberation/freedom so as to experience myself as the powerful being that I am. But in order for me to experience this, I would need to experience the opposite of this. In order to know love, one must know the opposite of it. And knowing the opposite will give rise to the desire to want to experience the opposite positive state.

This negative or opposite is what we would call the Core Wound. My Core Wound was the opposite of freedom and the opposite of Power – Powerlessness and Entrapment. And this negative core wound will repeat itself over and over again until we are able to recognize our core wound and its purpose in our lives.

In order to truly know and be aligned with our Souls Purpose, one must recognize, process and integrate our Core Wound. Our core wound is the ultimate thing we have come to overcome in order to experience our deepest desires.

What is your core wound?

What is the recurring overall negative feeling you have experienced all of your life that has given rise to your ultimate feeling goal now? In other words, what is the recurring, overall negative feeling you have experienced your whole life that has moved you, pushed you, inspired you to be the exact opposite? Maybe you've never experienced true unconditional love so you are moved to seek fulfilling love? Or maybe you've felt powerless, so you are moved to seek power? Whatever the case, become aware of your core pattern, as another cannot heal it.

Your core wound is part of your life's blueprint, which means it must be felt, recognized, processed and shifted by YOU.

The Manifestation of years of darkness, hidden trauma and abuse

I had no idea what would make me happy and I also didn't know what my purpose was. As the years had gone by, my life mirrored back to me all that was unhealed and fractured within me. It appeared in the relationships I attracted into my reality. Relationships that perpetuated abuse, feelings of worthlessness, disapproval and emptiness. These relationships would reflect all the aspects within me that needed resolution and integration. I finally came to see my search for the perfect man, who I hoped would make me whole and truly love me, was futile. Why? Because what I was really looking for, was myself.

My career had taken off, I was working in the financial industry as a Bank Manager, however I was anything but happy and fulfilled. I finally learned I had made the all-too-common mistake of thinking financial success would lead to me to contentment, happiness, and freedom.

But it didn't.

It was then I began to ask questions and seek answers.

And the first time I decided to seek a reading from a Psychic Clairvoyant I was in my early 20s, and I can remember very clearly what she had said, she said "It might sound cliché but your healing hands will lead you into the direction of healing". And these words stuck with me. I had never even thought of myself as a healer, never delved into any healing arts, never even thought these things were possible within the confines of the life that I knew.

A few days later, while researching how to quit smoking, I came across a web site called Healing Hands. The site suggested Hypnotherapy to stop smoking. Immediately I recognized the harmony with what the Psychic had said about healing hands.

I then embarked on this journey and became a certified Hypnotherapist, NLP practitioner and completed my Psychology Degree. This was the beginning of my healing and awakening journey and uncovering of my purpose. This was the day when a little light, was brought to my unconsciousness (sleep state and illusion).

I was the Creator – The Lesson of the Law of Attraction

"The very thing you resist the most, is the thing that's trying to draw you into the self. The very thing you resist the most is the invitation that's calling you into transformation. This thing is looking to enlighten you at this very moment. The relief you are seeking is already seeking you, yet the mind convinces you otherwise."

Riana Arendse

The idea is that by becoming conscious and aware about the fact that we create our realities, we in turn take back our power, activate or bring about a stronger desire within our lives, and by following that specific desire, we alter our vibration into something else, something more in alignment. Coming into a law of attraction-based reality is the ultimate course of self-awareness and expansion, which is why so many beings experience enlightenment here.

If you were abused when you were young and couldn't resolve it when it occurred, you grow up being a match to trauma. So, all you attract is more traumatizing experiences, as I have mentioned in my story.

There are also other common ways that a child can attract negative circumstances like abuse into their reality. This is when the child adopts negative energetic vibrations from his or her environment and then attracts those things which match that vibration into their own experience, their external reality.

Society creates beliefs and rules to define when a person is and isn't responsible for their lives. In the same way, we define the age in which a person has free will and the law of attraction can apply to them. The truth is, the law of attraction is working every single moment, on all aspects, all ages, and all dimensions in this universe. There is no pause button. Period.

There is also no pause button as far as vibration is concerned. Children adopt and take on and therefore present "vibrations" long before they have the ability to speak. Even whilst in the womb. Children adopt and offer thought well before their physical brains are developed. Thought is not a result of the brain; it is a result of universal consciousness. And so, they are attracting physical things which are a match to those vibrations even that early on in development. The expression of particular genetic factors or DNA is even the result of these early vibrations. Vibrations cannot be "imposed" from one life form to another, but they are a contributing factor. And the stronger the vibration is, the bigger the contributing factor is.

If a child for example comes into an environment of extreme worry, anxiety and fear, it is difficult for them to not adopt that same vibration of fear and worry. They have not consciously decided how they want to think about what they observe, they are simply observing. They have observed this fearful way of thinking and adopted it, which makes them now a match to things which reinforces that vibration. It makes them a match to other people who also hold the vibration of fear and powerlessness such as perpetrators. Perpetrators act out physically from the feeling of powerlessness and fear. Victims are also in the vibration of powerlessness and fear, but they do not act on it. They are still, despite the behavior and the action, identical energetic vibrations to each other. The child does not deserve it. It is not the child's fault. It is simply an effect of how the universe works with regards to vibration and the law of resonance or attraction.

The law of attraction should never be understood in terms of blame (i.e. "they brought it on themselves" or "it's their fault."). As this is not a statement of blame. To be clear, children DO NOT deserve to be victims of perpetrators. Abuse is NOT a child's fault.

Instead, what is accurate is to say that everything which ever happens to anyone, child or otherwise, is an exact match to the energetic vibration they hold. There is a similar vibrational frequency within both victim and perpetrator, on the basis of deep-seated emotion and beliefs.

The law of attraction then draws them to those things which are an exact match to those energetic vibrations, and it draws those things which are an exact match to those energetic vibrations to them and their external realities. These includes all relationships, friends, associates, jobs, opportunities, places, events, situations and communities. Once you come into physical life, most people, including children, do not know what energetic vibrations they are offering until they experience the physical manifestation of them. As you've seen in my story, the older I grew, the greater my subconscious projected into my external reality. This is not wrong. It just is, without judgment. And it can be changed at any moment.

There is no such thing as a childhood experience which a person cannot evolve and heal from. And even though childhood abuse is the direct result of having a matching negative vibration present in the child as well as the abuser, it is NOT a matter of fault and it is not a matter of the abuse being somehow deserved or justified.

When we enter this life, our egos (separate identities) are not formed yet. The ego is primarily formed in relation to others as we go about experiencing life, especially during the socialization process. This is how we learn the concepts of good and bad and right and wrong. Most importantly, we learn which aspects of our behavior are acceptable and unacceptable.

38

In time it becomes noticeably clear that love and reward come in response to what is suitable and acceptable, and abandonment and punishment come in response to what is unsuitable and unacceptable. As a result, we begin to ignore, deny, and suppress what we think is unacceptable and unsuitable about us. That is, we split our consciousness, divide ourselves, and become fractured. This division gives birth to the subconscious mind. To distinguish between the two minds, the subconscious mind can be called "the shadow" (because we cannot see it clearly and thus are not aware of it); and the conscious mind can be called the "the light" (because we can see it clearly and are aware of it).

Separation and division are not a natural state, it is an unhealed state and so the shadow aspect strives to be integrated again regardless of how much we wish that it would "go away or leave". The shadow activates whenever something in the subconscious is triggered into our awareness by a physical event or by circumstances in our life. For example, if our partner doesn't show up on time, which triggers a deeply suppressed feeling of abandonment that we are not even aware of, we might spend the next 45 minutes stressing out in what seems to be an enormous overreaction to the situation at hand.

Healing is nothing more than the process of making the unconscious conscious and the unacceptable, acceptable. And the integration of unconsciousness leads to complete and total awareness, which we will talk about later. People often think that "If you focus on your wounds and trauma all you will get is more pain". These arguments come from a very limited and elementary understanding and viewpoint of consciousness, resistance and The Law of Attraction.

People who have committed themselves and their healing practices to shadow work know from personal experience that over time less and less shadow work has to be done because you have become more and more integrated and more healed and whole. But there is a reason people avoid this healing modality. Shadow healing work (which I also refer to as "inner child healing") often leads to an initial emotional crisis. When you first gives yourself permission to open the door to your subconscious closet, your subconscious comes rushing out like flood water from a broken levee. Think of it as emotional purging. Because so much of you was deemed unacceptable and wrong while you were growing up, a great portion of you, yourself was banished to the subconscious mind. Because of this, a great deal of one's subconscious shadow needs to be integrated. When the purging process begins, it might feel like there is no end to the emerging shadow wounds. Every day there's a new shadow and you feel the same way you do when you have a stomach bug; like you're leaning over a toilet and you can't stop throwing up. It's easy and tempting to think that your life has gotten worse since you started the healing work. But this is a healing crisis. This is a purge. And in most cases, this is the point that most people stop doing the internal healing work and turn back from where they came, when it is actually the time that that an immense breakthrough wants to occur, instead of turning back, they would integrate if not attain an enlightenment experience. They would experience freedom and wholeness and peace for the very first time.

Why is it important to turn around and face your fears? Granted, purging requires facing your fears and that can be a scary idea. But facing your fears, rather than running from them, is the only way to ensure they no longer have power over you. If you keep running from your fears, like a ghost, your shadow will follow you to the ends of the earth, begging to be integrated with your light of consciousness, and no amount of positive focus will make it disappear. And long story short, focus upon the shadow does not create more shadow because the shadow that is exposed to the light of consciousness ceases to be a shadow.

How one's childhood plays a part in the coding of your Now reality

The reality is, you didn't incarnate into this life with all the conditioning, trauma, and limiting beliefs you may have now. You are the sum of your experiences and earlier conditioning due to the environment and upbringing you had. Even though there are certain frequencies and vibrational situations you opted into as part of incarnating here on this planet, most of the frequency you hold was created due to the social environment you had growing up, as well as the strong influence of your parents.

This is where all of the foundational programming was laid. In order to shift and heal aspects of your frequency that are out of alignment, you must return to the time the misalignment occurred and change it there. And what we are changing is not the actual experiences but how we processed those experiences and perceived them from the aspect of the little child.

When we are young, the adults around us grab our attention and feed us information through reiteration, repetition, and recurrence. This is how we gain knowledge, form beliefs, and come to see and perceive everything. It's also how we learn appropriate behavior, what is right and wrong, what is negative and positive, what is good and evil, and what is ugly and beautiful. By doing so, we learned a whole new reality, a whole new filter in which to see and perceive everything.

Even nurturing parents who have the greatest intentions of love and care can still create seriously defective programming in a child's mind—programming that can negatively affect the child throughout his or her life, until their misaligned frequency is shifted or healed.

This universe always pairs parents with children who hold the key to their self-awareness, healing and expansion. This is a child who is supposed to switch a parent's patterns to be in alignment with the parent's actual desires. Parents either both realize this and shift or resist that shift and by doing so, turn against their own child. In other words, a child serves as a conduit or trigger for their parents in order for the parent to heal and then get into alignment with their own desires. The child gives the parent an opportunity to re-parent their inner child. In other words, Children are actually the parent's biggest teacher. In essence a parent will be given a child who will be in conflict with the parent's negative pattern so as to help them reach their innate desires.

For example, a father really wants freedom in life but has a negative pattern or belief of scarcity, so he takes any job he can find, even at the expense of his own happiness. He then has a child who would rather be unemployed than work in a job that makes him unhappy. This angers the father. The father doesn't see the child has come to free him from his limiting beliefs so he can shift his negative pattern and achieve the freedom he seeks, which is his true inner desire.

And so, the father is triggered because he is not living his truth as a soul. So, whether you want to admit it or not, it doesn't matter whether or not they intended to do it, your parents and the social conditioning you went through, and the early life experiences you had, were the basis for your problems in your life. Accepting this and changing those patterns does not mean you are betraying your parents. In order to truly awaken we must be willing look at both negative and positive aspects of our parents.

After you no longer live with your parents and are no longer under the influence of their direct programming so to speak, the problem is no longer your parents. It is your parents residing within you that is the problem. Let me explain. Your parents are inside you. It is not your external parents that keep the detrimental pattern alive. It is your parents internalized. But the truth is you do not need to try and resolve the relationship with your parent, as they might or might not be willing to resolve or look at themselves, your healing has literally nothing to do with them. All you need to do is improve the relationship happening between the internalized parts of you that are a reflection of your parents and whatever parts are opposite of those parts of you (the parts they oppose). The reality is that most of you who are still telling the story that your childhood was great or at least good, are avoiding looking at your own faulty programming because of fear. And that fear is perfectly understandable...However, know this, your past does not dictate your future because free will is an absolute of your existence. It is possible to break out of the path of determinism with conscious awareness and healing. It is possible to change these patterns you have been programmed with. To do it, you need to change the pattern within your parents within yourself.

One of the main barriers to spiritual awakening, enlightenment, or self-realization is our unhealed relationships with our parents, whether they are living or not.

If your parents evoke resentment, shame, anger, guilt, abandonment, regret, blame, or fear, again, learn to welcome it because it is showing you where you are not yet free. We will get into the actual process of Un-becoming, healing and self-mastery a bit later on in this book. If you follow the process, you will begin to clear and heal your inner child wounds.

CHAPTER 2:

My Awakening

Consciousness was Uncomfortable

"The awareness that there is nothing you can do is the most important realization you can have. Because then we are no longer fixed within that which is known. We begin to see that life can take care of itself that in fact it's always taking care of itself. When we're lost in the complexities of our thinking, we become unconscious of the effortless flow of life, but life which is constantly revealing itself, which is ever changing, always making itself known, never remaining as any one thing as awakened consciousness; is operating all the time in its unending flow."

Riana Arendse

What is Spiritual Awakening?

The spiritual awakening process is inner transformation during which the way you think and experience life, changes. There is no return ticket and the life as you knew it disappears. The spiritual awakening process begins with a quiet voice in your head asking you: Is there more to life? Why am I here? Is it too late or am I just too scared to change?

Before you know it, your thoughts become deeper. You re-evaluate your relationships and also your life purpose. Gradually your heart opens up, and your feelings intensify to the point that it becomes challenging to suppress them. I'm sure if you're reading those lines that you're in the process of spiritual awakening because otherwise you wouldn't have felt attracted to the topic of this book.

Spiritual awakening is an awakening of an aspect of one's reality beyond the confines of the ego. The ego is our exclusive or separate sense of self or "I." This Spiritual awakening occurs when, for whatever reason, the ego somehow let's go completely so that a Higher Self or Spirit can arise within. While the ego is always doing, the Spirit remains forever in a state of being. As the process of spiritual awakening unfolds, the ego begins to redirect to the Spirit. Some might experience a single moment of spiritual awakening. But for most of us, this doesn't generally happen in a single "moment of awakening." While we can have "peak experiences" that open us up to divine reality, these experiences tend to be fleeting for most of us. Instead, in most cases including mine, we go through stages and phases of spiritual growth. And these permanent stages tend to develop over time.

There tends to be a few myths when it comes to awakening and one of these myths are that one must always strive to go towards love, peace and light, but in truth, spiritual awakening comes from the opposite direction where we face the fear, anger, guilt, and grief stored in us since childhood. Coming to terms with these experiences paves the way for authentic spiritual development.

Spiritual experiences are overwhelmingly positive experiences. They are experiences of heaven, in which we perceive reality at a heightened intensity, feel a powerful sense of inner well-being, experience a sense of oneness with our surroundings and become aware of a force of benevolence and harmony which permeates all that is. When the experience is especially intense, the whole world may dissolve into an ocean of blissful spiritual light, which we realize is the ground of all reality, the source from which the world has arisen, and the true nature of our being.

It might seem paradoxical that spiritual experiences are often triggered by states of intense despair, depression, pain, or mental and emotional turmoil. I have observed many examples of such transformational experiences during my work as a healer and teacher. A few examples: an alcoholic who reached 'rock bottom' and lost everything but then became liberated; a woman who has lived in a state of wakefulness ever since being told she had a terminal illness; and a man who struggled for months with pain and despair and one day had a near death experience, then underwent a complete spiritual rebirth and now lives in a state of permanent bliss. Myself, when suffering immense sexual and emotional trauma from a very young age and then in my early adulthood having my spiritual awakening experience.

These people are every-day-people who experienced a "point of transformation" when they stopped resisting their predicament, their pain, their situation(s), and completely let go. They underwent a shift in consciousness, after which they lived—and still live—in a constant state of well-being and a constant "attitude of gratitude" about the basic good of life, a new connection to the Divine, and a new life meaning and purpose. It's also very significant that many great spiritual teachers have found enlightenment after intense periods of mental and emotional torment. The contemporary spiritual teacher and author Eckhart Tolle had a similar awakening experience. He writes that until his thirtieth year he lived with anxiety and suicidal depression. One night he woke up with 'a feeling of absolute dread' inside him and felt a strong desire to kill himself. This triggered a powerful spiritual experience, in which he was 'drawn into what seemed like a vortex of energy,' and which led to a state of enlightenment:

In my view, spiritual experiences induced by despair or mental turmoil are what is most common today, even in my story. However, the key to understanding the experiences is the concept of attachment, the concept of one's personal mind made story. Normally, as human beings we are psychologically attached to a large number of constructs, such as hopes and ambitions for the future, beliefs and ideas concerning life, concerning who we are or who we think we are and the world, our internal story about ourselves and our experiences, the knowledge we have accumulated, and our image of ourselves, including our sense of status, our appearance and accomplishments and achievements. These are accessories which become attached to the sense of self, but which are not actually a part of our true nature. At the same time, there are more tangible attachments, such as possessions, jobs, and other human beings whose approval and attention we might need or want. These are the building blocks of the ego. We feel that we are 'someone' because we have hopes, beliefs, status, a job and possessions and because other people give us approval. However, in states of despair and depression all – or at least some of – these attachments are broken. This is the very reason why you are in despair: because the constructs you've been depending for your well-being have been removed; the 'bridge' which supported your sense of identity has fallen away. Hopes and beliefs are revealed as illusions; your possessions and status have been taken away, your friends or lovers have rejected you. This loss of sense of self, this loss of identity, or loss of the idea of yourself and how you wanted things to be, must leave in order for you to truly Un-become. It is a gift or blessing in disguise as one would say. As a result, you feel naked and lost, as if your identity has been destroyed. But at this very point you are, paradoxically, close to a state of liberation. You are in a state of detachment. Your Self has been released from external constructs.

In an instant of surrender, the pain of despair and anguish can switch into a state of freedom and joy. For some it is temporary or passing (like a layer had been shed) and for others permanent (like a whole bigger part has been shed).This may also be why some severe alcoholics and other addicts have powerful awakening experiences when they reach 'rock bottom', when their addiction has destroyed their lives and they can no longer sustain themselves with hopes or illusions or their mind made stories. This is also why encountering death is such a powerful trigger of spiritual experiences. Like states of despair and depression, facing death may occasionally induce a state of detachment, in which the individual spontaneously releases herself from attachments and just surrender to the Divine.

Such realizations can also occur after a person is diagnosed with a fatal illness and is told they only have a certain amount of time left to live. Initially he or she experiences feelings of bitterness and despair, which may give way to a sense of serenity and acceptance and a new spiritual perception.

This is why, initially at least, facing death is a painful experience. You are stripped of the externalities which give you your sense of identity, security and well-being. You are literally reduced to nothing. Many people do not move beyond this pain; for them the process of pain or suffering is simply a depressing and devastating experience, not redeemed by any sense of joy or meaning. But for some people this state of enforced detachment brings about a shift to a spiritual state. As the attachments dissolve, there is a sudden intensification and stilling of life-energy, enabling the dying or suffering person to look at the world with fresh, child-like vision, to experience serenity and peace inside, and to become aware of their essential oneness with everything.

So, where does this leave us?

Does it mean that we must suffer in order to have spiritual experiences or become enlightened? Do we have to make our lives as empty and miserable as possible, to renounce the world, take vows of silence and live minimally?

Of course, not – there is a 'middle way' between this extreme suffering and a life of attachment. As we live our lives, we should try to make sure that we don't become too dependent upon externalities like money, status, hopes, beliefs, our self-image and other people. We should try to make sure that we're always partly rooted inside ourselves, so that we never give ourselves completely away to things that are temporary and passing. We should remember that the only true source of well-being lies inside us, and that to attach ourselves to externalities means losing touch with this. Through making a conscious effort to remain self-sufficient and connected to our true selves, our beings will be open and free, and there will always be space for Spirit to flow through.

Only by realizing the truth of things are things set right. If we are lucky, we get disillusioned so badly that the experiences of Life tend to help us to rid and free ourselves of that which is not real. The hardship and pain we experience makes it so that we tend to wake up just a bit faster than the rest. This may not seem "lucky," but nothing awakens us faster than hardship and pain.

The awakening comes directly from God/Source, to prod the part that is still asleep and unconscious, known as you, awake.

What is really true, why am I here, why does life feel so empty of true meaning?

These very important questions are the beginning, the start, the thorn in the mind and the motivation, for waking up out of illusion, out of unconsciousness. For the soul experiencing a spiritual awakening, this opens the final door to liberation; from the belief of "I am this or that," to the realization of "I am." A spiritual awakening creates a "no turning back" point in our lives. Once we've awakened, there's no way to return to the old you. It's like a butterfly trying to fit back into the cocoon and re-join her old caterpillar friends. It just can't happen. But as soon as she grows accustomed to her wings, she'll discover that flying is much better than crawling. If you're going through a spiritual awakening, the following are some points to help you recognize the various emotions you may be experiencing now.

1. You begin question everything.

You will begin to examine what you've been taught to believe. This can feel isolating because it's our beliefs that comfort us. But you will soon start to see that truth is much more liberating than illusions. Often, it's a period of loss or suffering that precipitates this questioning period.

2. Wanting to know your purpose.

Why am I here? This is one of the deepest questions an awakener must ask. As you're busy investigating what you believe versus what you now know to be true, take time to explore yourself. During this awakening, you will develop a hungry desire for a deeper understanding of who you are and why you're here. Begin the "un-becoming process;" remove all labels we blanket ourselves in. If you aren't a doctor, a dad, a cleaner, a teacher, a volunteer, a sister or brother, who are you? As you find the courage to remove your labels, you will discover who you really are and during this solitary journey, the treasure you'll find is your soul purpose.

3. You become more independent.

People who are waking up no longer feel the need to fit in and belong. This is not an overnight realization, so be gentle with yourself as you begin to understand that the very words "fitting in" connote feelings of being trapped, boxed in. You're a free soul and have the divine right to think, feel and believe what you want. During this time, you may move away from groups or organizations that no longer matter to you.

Again, the message here is patience. Be patient with yourself but also with those around you who may not understand why you're changing and shifting.

4. Old friendships/relationships shift and change.

One of the hardest parts of going through a spiritual awakening is that many of our relationships begin to shift, change or even end. This can lead to feelings of loss, fear, and loneliness. Your friends may not understand this new you and will begin to question or challenge you. Everyone has a right to their opinion and when you defend your views, you're only contributing to the dualistic divide from which you're rising from. Listen to your friends. Hear their concerns. Meet them with compassion. Some of them will walk away but many will stay. You will also start to meet new friends who are in alignment with your awakening consciousness.

5. You lose interest in material things.

We all need to work and most of us enjoy shopping for new, shiny things. But as you go through your spiritual awakening, this will become less and less important. This is often called the "Minimalist Stage." You may start to clear out your closets, donate old clothes, bikes and furniture. You start to see how little you really need in order to feel happy and present. Your goals may shift now from getting that new promotion or saving up for that new house to achieving inner joy, healing or spending more time with loved ones and learning to live each day in gratitude and awareness.

6. You have intense joy followed by total loneliness.

This is one of the hardest stages of the spiritual awakening. As you start to see the world as connected and whole, you feel a sense of profound joy that we are eternal beings, that our energy is linked with all those around us, and that we can co-create with the Universe. But just as you're settling into this ecstasy, you will be hit with a powerful sense of loneliness, possibly even a sense of uselessness. Feel your way through this up and down period. No emotion will last forever. You're saying goodbye to aspects of yourself that no longer serve you. It's very similar to the grief process. When you realize how most people no longer understand you or even support you in your awakening, you may feel isolated and think about going back to the "old you." The message here is again one of patience. When the butterfly emerges from the cocoon, she's not ready to fly. She must give her wings time to acclimate to the climate. Remind yourself during this stage "This too shall pass" and soon you'll be soaring.

7. You feel compassion for all beings.

As you start to see, feel and sense the unified energy flowing through all living beings, you begin to feel love and compassion for all humans, animals and living things on our planet. This will alter the way you see the news, interact with those around you and how you treat animals and the planet. You may start to recycle more, pick up trash as you take your daily walk or even change your eating habits. As you reach this stage of compassion, much of the difficulties and sense of loneliness will start to dissipate. You will see yourself as a soul have a human experience. You will start to engage with others through an energy of love which will dramatically alter and enhance your interactions and all your experiences. You are now ready to fly.

8. Spiritual Un-Becoming, you feel like you are losing yourself. This means to gradually become naked, emptying the soul so that the fullness of the spirit can enter. Shedding all old beliefs, opinions, stories, personas, judgements. Everything that isn't true will begin to go. And this process can be painful but liberating in all its glory.

Spiritual Awakening is a path that leads to our inherent nature of enlightenment, if we are courageous enough to let go and allow. It's about moving away from attaching ourselves to wanting but rather than knowing our power and choosing that which we want. Wanting and Choosing are 2 different vibrations, one stems from a place of need or lack and the other from a place of knowing. Knowing is the key to mastery. Because in knowing, you already are, and you already have. Knowing is beyond trust or faith, it is absolute and concrete. It is unshakeable.

Can we rise above identifications with form (the physical) that keeps ego in place? The possibility of such transformation has always been an integral message of the great teachings of all masters and messengers of the past and present.

Believing that you are a separate person, hurts.

From beautiful awakening back to familiar dilemma

During your spiritual awakening, there will be pivotal moments when you experience feelings of internal death or even physical loss of sorts. After my own most pivotal spiritual awakening moment, I lost my job and was unemployed, which was scary because I had a house, car, bills, and parents to support. But at that moment of internal death and outer loss, the Divine whispered truths in my ear that shocked me, but also brought me to remembrance.

Yes, deep within my core, I remembered and woke up out of my sleep state of illusion I had been living all my life. For the first time, I understood how every past experience I endured had led to that very moment, the moment I started stepping into the truth of who I truly am. It felt as if I had awakened up from a dream.

Spirituality is the willingness to completely fail, the willingness to completely be brought to your knees. It's the willingness to be courageous enough to completely face yourself, both light and dark aspects - because even reaching a point of enlightenment still requires integration. That's why, although my friends, clients and students think I've figured out something masterful and wonderful, I tell them all the time: my path was the path of suffering, of struggle, a path of failure, internal death and absolute defeat. Everything I tried I failed at, even to this day life needed to show me extremely big lessons and dissolve many illusions and hurts.

I want to share with you one of the most beautiful experiences that I've ever had. It occurred during my spiritual awakening. As I was sitting down quietly, listening to the sounds of the night. As I looked up at the white walls and ceiling encircling me, I was suddenly overcome with a strange sense of "waking up" from a very long and intricate dream that I had been taking part of for my entire life. The room I was in, seemed to merge with me like there was no "self" or "I," just an unfathomable vastness, an endless wholeness. For those few moments, everything was an expression of perfection and underneath all that I saw was an infinite stillness and silence; a purity of unity. I was everything and everything was me. And it was in that moment that everything I have ever looked for, everything I have ever intuitively sensed and desired, was fulfilled.

Here's what I have taken away from that experience to share with you: When we begin our spiritual journeys of inner growth, we discover many things about ourselves, other people and the world. We uncover the lies we tell ourselves and others, the lies the world tells us, we work on exploring our personalities, we work on improving our personalities, we heal our wounds, we try to make peace with ourselves, we try to make amends with others ... and many more things that go hand-in-hand with the cultivation of self-awareness, self-discovery, self-understanding and self-transformation. These are all very useful practices.

Eventually, we develop a pretty good understanding of ourselves —of our core wounds and shadow elements and of our true dreams and gifts. We nourish our bodies, change our diets, create healthy personal boundaries, cut away toxic habits, say goodbye to destructive people, build new friendships and relationships, and eventually develop love and respect for who we think we are. This is all imperative.

And yet, after all that amazing transformative progress, chances are you will find yourself facing a familiar dilemma: You will still feel as though something is missing in your life. That you still haven't done enough. That you still aren't enough. Why? Because the awakening process is a shedding process, and only the first step on the journey to "oneness," which I will discuss shortly.

We still work to pursue creating an "ideal self," that always feels happy, that never suffers and that is constantly at peace. We still work to build and enhance our identities, whether through identifying as Vegans, as Yogis, as Empaths, as Intuitives, as Buddhists, as Healers, as Spiritual Students or Teachers, as Old Souls, as Shamans, and as any of the other labels we love to collect and embody. And yet ... we are never happy. We always seek more – we always seek to "be" more. Our quest is never-ending. We think that we can "defeat" the mind by using the mind ... but have you ever questioned the validity of this?

Discovering you are an expression of Oneness

Who is this that who is never satisfied, never happy, never feeling like they are enough?

Have you ever asked yourself the following question?

"Will I ever be enough?"

"Will You Every Really Be Enough"?

The question may seem silly: "Of course I am enough!" you might think as I once did. "I am a smart, beautiful, intelligent, kind and loving person – of course I am enough!"

Yes, yes you are. And to achieve this kind of self-respect is an important part of the spiritual development and growth process away from self-hatred to self-love. But there comes a time after you have cultivated self-love and self-respect where you come to realize something miraculous:

You will never be enough because who you "think" you are is not truly "who" you are. Yes, allow me to say that again: You will never be enough because who you think you are is not truly who you are.

All of the memories, all of the beliefs, all of the associations, all of the spiritual and worldly labels, all of the tastes, all of the traumas, all of the loves and hates, all of the insecurities and strengths, they are not truly "who" you are. And no matter how highly you regard yourself, no matter how popular, liked, celebrated, or lovable you are — your identity remains as a burden; a barrier that prevents you from the purest self-realization which is that you are an expression of Oneness. Your true nature has no name, no form, no identity, and no limits. You are everything and nothing at the same time. And that is what this book is about, it is about un-becoming, truly stripping away every single thing that is not truth. Because the awakening process or experience in most cases does not eradicate these things automatically, it is a shedding process, of removing and not adding.

Here are five of the most powerful questions you can ask yourself at any moment to help you finally realize and embrace who you truly are:

Am I this emotion?

Am I this thought?

Am I this body?

Am I this personality?

Who am I?

At first these questions might sound strange, overly simplistic, and even bizarre. But the more self-aware you become of your thought processes which give birth to your feelings, perceptions, assumptions and beliefs about the world, the more you will come to see how closely you identify with all of these elements. All of which are transient and subject to change and therefore not reliable), the more you will be able to identify how they define your identity and, most importantly, begin stripping them away

When I first started asking these questions, I was immediately uncomfortable and unwilling to completely follow through all the way to the end with such self-inquiry. I thought, "If I'm not this emotion, thought, physical sensation, experience, circumstance, body and personality because they are all transient and subject to growth, change and decay ... what am I?"

My conclusion was, "I am none of these things – I am nothing!" And because of my dark and miserly associations with the word "nothing," I have neglected to ask these questions seriously. But I have since experienced otherwise. I have discovered the truth which is that being "nothing" is paradoxically being everything. Being empty of your fabricated identity is paradoxically being completely full and whole again. Far from being desolate and void, being "nothing" is existing in a state of immense rest, of endless peace and profound liberation.

Once you investigate the true depths of the question, "Who am I?" you come to a fascinating realization: "you" are not who you think you are, what you assume you are, what you have been taught you are, or what you have come to believe you are, and you never have been.

Why? Because all these things are temporary and thus passing; yet you, your essence, still remain.

Consciousness was Uncomfortable.

What is consciousness?

Up to this point, we have been discussing the necessity of surrender, of letting go, to strip our worldly attachments away so we can discover our purpose and experience rest, peace, and freedom. Now we can move into a discussion on consciousness, which is active awareness of our spiritual essence and being, of our core self.

From healing and spiritual awakening, we awaken from unconsciousness to active consciousness.

Consciousness becomes an awareness that we have a higher self, core Self, Heart, which is our essence, our true reality, but that core self-dwells in this physical realm inhabiting this body. The awareness of Heart, Presence, essential Spirit, within our body initiates consciousness. It's about as simple as that.

When we awaken to this essence, when we become aware of higher Self, we realize all others also have that same essence, whether awakened, aware, conscious, or not. It's an energy of understanding, acceptance, and love — of self and others. After waking out of unconsciousness, we don't just sit back and allow bad things. But we do understand why they happen. And this opens the door to forgiveness because we realise that everything happens according to the level of consciousness of the people involved. We still have feelings, thoughts, emotions, but we 'see' them in a new way. We realise what they are, and they no longer take us over. We don't get caught up in them and they don't linger with us or become obsessive. Difficult emotions are seen for what they are, and lose their strength, because we know where they come from – being unconsciousness. When unconscious we react, behave, think, do, according to what we believe we need and want. The vast majority of us have certain beliefs and almost exclusively rely our mind for guidance in how we live our lives - but this is living unconsciously.

What it means to be Unconscious

Well, until you have had a glimpse of something else, a different dimension that includes a strong intuitive sense of an inner knowing that one's mind is not all there is to you, so to speak, it will be impossible for words to convey the essence of an explanation. But we can point to understanding.

We base our decision making and response to all that we encounter in our daily lives on what we have become accustomed to believing. In other words, our knowledge and experience. So we relate everything to what has come before, to the past, our memories, everything that has happened to us, and this causes all kinds of trouble because when doing this we are closed to what is fresh and new in the now moment. Another way of putting this is that we automatically go inside our heads for our response to the world. How limited is that! But it is the norm. In our heads then we have created this idea of knowledge, based on accumulated stuff, and we see this as our personality. As a result, we take everything personally and reacted accordingly. But if we take a look at it, how small a perspective is that?

Once we realise that all thinking and emotion is happening within the space of who we are, we are becoming conscious of the reality we previously had never even been aware existed.

Once we realise that our previous 'normal' state, that almost everyone is still in, is as unconscious as we were, we stop being affected so much by everything that others do. We become able to see that until we come out of unconsciousness, we act according to a very limited mind-conditioned sense of self. Once we become conscious of this, we start to accept people as they are, and forgiveness happens naturally. A deeply unconscious person can justify anything to themselves. After waking out of unconsciousness, we don't just sit back and allow bad things. But we do understand why they happen. Most importantly, when we understand how they could commit evil acts, they no longer have power or control over us.

And this opens the door to forgiveness because we realise that everything happens according to the level of consciousness of the people involved. We still have feelings, thoughts, emotions, but we 'see' them in a new way. We realise what they are, and they no longer take us over. We don't get caught up in them and they don't linger with us or become obsessive.

Consciousness is our true nature. It is the freedom in which life happens to us. Difficult emotions are seen for what they are, and lose their strength, because we know where they come from – unconsciousness. This waking out of unconsciousness is a huge leap. But paradoxically, it is no leap at all. The deeper and wider aspect of self, this omnipotent presence has always been there but is obscured by the constant mind-stream and all the associated emotions. Those who come to this understanding have often first experienced deeply painful life events as mentioned before, which have driven them seek answers. They have gone inwards through meditation and other practices or have sought out spiritual knowledge through books and teachers. Unconsciousness is the reason and basis for our bondage, which makes us move in circles and takes us nowhere.

The answer, and the only way to become free from the mental and emotional suffering of life experiences, is to finally realise that we are not who we think we are! We are not our accumulated beliefs, memories, ideas. These are just energy patterns within our bodies. We are so much more than them! All of us have experienced moments of being conscious.

Do you remember these moments?

When you were just completely present in the moment?
Completely and utterly operating from the heart?

The moment when you stare into your new-born baby's eyes, or the moment you stop to take in the beauty of nature.

These are the moments when you are fully present, fully in the heart centre, fully embodying your God essence, fully present in the now.

The now is the only thing that is true.

When you can recognize your own unconsciousness that in and of itself is - awakening. Being able to recognize one's own dysfunction is the very first crucial step in elevating your consciousness and the beginning of healing.

Along this path of awakening, you are going to have to truly face yourselves, all aspects of you. And I won't feel good to see things about ourselves that we don't want to see. It doesn't feel good to recognize truths that we don't want to be true. And even though it didn't feel good at times, and I personally felt I was dying on the inside, my entire identity slipping away, all illusions revealing themselves; however, my pursuit for the absolute Truth was always more important than any comfortableness or happiness.

In my most painful awakening in this life, I spent days, weeks and months being forced to accommodate and integrate all the things I didn't want and hated as part of myself. My mother being a witness could attest to this. There were moments I had wished I could go back to living an illusion in order to just find some relief...But the truest part of me knew, there was no turning back now, nor would I really ever want to. I then had to completely accept all of these parts as myself.

Life brought me straight to my knees.

There was nothing more I could hold on to, all that was left to do was just Let Go, fall into the Abyss, into the Void.

There was NOTHING left. And even though I had failed many times, it didn't mean that the trying and effort didn't play an important role. The struggle did play a role. But it was influential, because it got me to an end of that role that I was playing. The Roles, false sense of self, masks and personas all began to discard. I failed until it all was extinguished. I Danced the Dance until all was dissolved. Until the music stopped.... But I failed...painfully, truly and absolutely - failed. I failed at being positive, I failed at meditating well, I failed at being awareness, I failed at healing, I failed at figuring out the truth. Everything that I used to succeed spiritually failed. But at that moment of failure, that's when everything opened and revealed itself. These were the moments I knew a great shift had taken place.

These were the moments I experienced true Liberation, for the first time in all my resistant life.

Now these so called negative experiences, these darker moments that propels you into fear, loss, anxiety and anger, are only really created to propel you into change and to give you an opportunity for rapid expansion. These situations are not always kind to the ego or to the constructs that were made to protect it. However it is created for you by you, to propel you into a higher consciousness and higher realization of who you truly are.

The one thing we must remain aware of is the fact that everything is impermanent, and ever changing. Our properties, jobs, health, security are all just temporary and transient. And the only thing that remains is you. Your true essence is what will always remain. And it is more beneficial to learn to embrace these changes as wonderful opportunities to trust the power already within you. When you begin to move out of survival or fear mode and manifest the frequency of God in a situation.

Everything transforms.

From Fiction to Nonfiction:

Since my arrival as mentioned before, we are taught so many things growing up. What we need to be and what we need to have. What is good, what is bad, acceptable and unacceptable. We are also taught about history, about God, about this world we live in. And as I began awakening to the truth of who I truly was, the Divine bestowed upon me truths that I would have never ever thought possible. Even though I had gone through a phase of shock, these truths felt like truth, it completely resonated. I remembered and awakened to the fact that what was taught to me was just man-made truths, beliefs and it was a creation by man for man. I was shown that there was so much more that I purposefully forgot when I incarnated into this reality.

There was not only this world and this universe but there were many other worlds and universes out there. Other dimensions and other realities.

To explain the universe (even this one we are a part of) would be impossible because we are only seeing this universe through the lens of third dimensional language when I write these words to you now. So, it must be understood that these words only serve as a bridge that to the true experience of the multidimensional nature of our universe and other universes.

Every cell in your body is an individual perspective within the unified consciousness that we call source or god. And so, every cell in your body has multi-dimensional aspects and every cell in your body creates multi-dimensional realities. Play that out in your mind for a minute. There are more realities in this universe (and multi-dimensional ones at that), than a human mind could ever conceive of, because that is not the job of the human mind. The job of the human mind is to manage the human perspective.

I have remembered and experienced beings from other worlds and planets, some less evolved and others more evolved. I received these downloads of information and remembrances, however later along my journey I too experienced them.

The more highly evolved beings live from a place of complete oneness, there is no separation there. Social evolution is demonstrated by movement towards unity, not separatism. Unity is the absolute truth in those dimensions. In the realm of the absolute of all that is, we are all one. Not as in our world, where everything is built on duality. We imagine ourselves to be separate from each other. And this is depicted in separate religions, separate nations, separate people, separate clans and countries. And this separateness which is an illusion is the root of all the suffering on earth. The consciousness of separation in our world, is what creates most of our worldly so called negative experiences.

I met my spiritual guides, which consisted of my late grandmother (who I never met in this physical plane), Archangels, star beings (some known as the pleiadean and syrian people), and ascended masters (such as Jesus, Mother Mary, Mary Magdalene, Isis, and others) I remembered that I had lived thousands of past lives before, where I was still carrying old vows of poverty and vows of staying small, oaths, programmes and beliefs still present within my DNA, which also still needed to be released and healed.

And for me it was shocking but yet an inner remembrance of what I already knew. And so, my whole world changed. Everything I ever knew or was conditioned to believe was not true. And my journey of Un-becoming continued. I purged myself from all old constructs, beliefs and ways of seeing things. And this didn't happen overnight, because most of these beliefs are subconscious or hidden beliefs and others are stored within my DNA. And now that I knew that I and everyone else were divine powerful beings I had to figure out how to Un-become and reset my blueprint so to speak. I needed to learn how to remove old beliefs, programmes and traumas from my field and from my subconscious mind, in order for me to begin embodying my divinity and step into my true essence. As my true essence was always there...it was just stuck beneath all these superficial untruths.

Liberation through forgiveness

As I alluded to earlier, forgiveness is a major part of the Un-becoming equation. I forgave my perpetrators and I forgave myself. Why? You might ask.

I awakened to the truth that my dark past, pain, suffering and trauma, allowed me to find my purpose. And when I had my spiritual awakening, I realized the vibration and beliefs I previously held (during the years of abuse) matched those of my abusers. In other words, I realized I was just a victim of other victims. That the amount of pain, emotional disconnection, emotional invalidation, abuse or torment they must have endured as children too played a major role in them becoming perpetrators in later years.

Forgiveness, simply defined, is the letting go of blame or resentment toward anybody who has hurt, offended, or slighted you in the past. One of the keys to love and forgiveness is realizing the people who hurt you are only acting out of their own belief systems, their own stories of need and suffering. But with the light of consciousness and timeless awareness behind it, love is always unconditional.

I was no longer in my emotions but a witness and observer to what was really trying to unfold.

Take the unconditional perspective, and your love will be unconditional.

For many people the idea of forgiving someone who has abused them and devastated their life is totally unacceptable – even repulsive. Why forgive someone who has deliberately caused you untold amounts of pain and suffering? Surely forgiving means you will lose even more power to your abuser.

Learning to love and forgive ourselves for the ways in which we have failed to perform, or have harmed someone, or haven't measured up to our own high expectations, is extremely important on this path of awakening. Forgiveness really does start within. The most accurate gauge of how present and inwardly free we are is in our ability to connect with not just our parents, who may have hurt us, or people we may have harmed, but anybody, without fear or judgment, in a relaxed, nonthreatening way. Our look is open and welcoming. We have nothing to hide or prove.

To forgive someone is to give up feeling resentment, anger or the need for requital that you hold in relation to someone or something that you feel has hurt you. Forgiveness implies profound healing must take place. And when you walk the path of healing, forgiveness is something that happens to you and often quite spontaneously. It is as if forgiveness falls in your lap as a result of taking previous and seemingly unrelated steps on the healing path. If you look at people who have truly forgiven, you will find that you are looking at someone who is already living out the healed state of themselves. For example, I perceived that I had lost my whole childhood and would never get it back due to my childhood abusers. In my case, in order to heal, I had to grieve for that lost childhood and go back and give my inner child what she so longed for back then.

Look at everything in life, then, from the Whole, rather than from the parts. Getting the bigger picture was a major result of me facing the truth of my reality. I finally saw things from a bird's eye perspective, and this shifted everything for me. I remembered an important truth when I awakened, and that was that each and every person I encountered whether negative or positive, were just playing a role in my expansion. A role which was predestined and agreed to before I incarnated here. Encounters and situations which was called unto me by me. Agreements between souls to help each other to aid in their spiritual expansion and remembrance of who we truly are.

If you have a hard time thinking of things you love about the person you want to forgive, you can call on the valuable lessons you've learned from difficult times you experienced. On a soul level there are never victims and perpetrators, on a soul level there are only two or more souls who agreed to help each other in their soul growth. The soul will never condemn that which is deemed as negative but will bless it – seeing in it a part of itself, which must exist in order for another part of itself to manifest.

The practice here is to look at everything directly and accept it as your own creation.

Because it is.

Channelled Text and Clearing Activation

While writing this book, Spirit decided to intervene and wanted to channel a clearing of fear. The following text is written as channelled through me from a collective consciousness known as the ascended masters. The words itself is infused with a higher vibration of unconditional love, healing and energetic activations, which will allow the emotion and belief of fear to begin to release.

Do not read this unless you wish to be attuned or unless you feel called to do so:

The channelled text appears from this point to the end of the chapter.

First I would like to give you some idea of who the ascended Masters are and what their purpose is to humanity.

The ascended masters are essentially thought forms (personalities) that are being fed by universal consciousness (God/Source) for the benefit of the ascension and expansion of mankind. Source uses these specific thought forms or personalities because we relate to them. We have a collective desire for assistance and a collective association with these beings. And we identify with them to the degree that they are even being fed by the focus of our individual and collective consciousness, making these very powerful discarnate beings. The ascended masters assist the expansion of the consciousness of the human world or mankind at large.

We choose to incarnate into life after life until incarnation no longer serves our own expansion of the universe's expansion at large. Then, we either remain part of universal consciousness or we choose to incarnate in other time space realities, or we choose to take on the perspective of assisting other beings in their expansion process.

It is common that once one achieves the ability to line up with universal consciousness (often referred to as source mind) at will, this is the point at which a soul stream opts to make this transition out of the cycle of death and birth. The ascended masters are personalities that have left the cycle of death and birth, which is why they are referred to as ascended.

When viewed through the lens of linear time some of them are seen as recent additions, some are ancient and some are so old they have been forgotten. In truth, there are thousands or more of these beings called ascended masters. But some are the most active and widely recognized in today's age. An example of just a few of these ascended masters are: Saint Germain, Buddah, Jesus, Sana Kumara, Quan yin,

Metatron, Moses and Mother Mary. Because they are guides that assist mankind, you can expect to encounter them over the course of your spiritual journey in one way or another.

Beginning of Channelling:

Yes, today dear ones, we are going to focus on clearing the vibration of fear. We are going to be channelling as a consciousness you know as the ascended masters.

Fear has been the basis and only thing that humanity lives from, and because of this we are not able to fully live in love. As we are.

We want to make it very clear that there's no such thing as evil, there's only this very small perspective in our entire existence of God that thinks or perceives of something as evil.

One tiny dot within the whole entire universe of universes has the PERCEPTION of fear or evil. So, it really doesn't exist. If you really know that and really get that truth, you will not fear it. Everything single thing is LOVE. Period.

This vibration of fear and evil can be switched and released in the blink of an eye. Yes this is so.

The only thing that ever hinders us is fear. It doesn't matter what you do, the only thing that will ever hinder you is fear. That's it.

The having of a fear is much greater than the actual thing you fear. Every single thing in the entire universe is made up of the exact same thing, the exact same energy. You can either perceive it from a limited perspective or from an objective or universal viewpoint. There is absolutely nothing outside of you holding you back, the only thing holding you back is your fear. Your fear of anything, will hold you in that place of stuckness.

In every instance you can choose to see things from the perspective of God instead of from the small self. These things might seem bad to you but if you step back and see things from a greater view, a greater picture, you will see that everything is in divine order. Just as it should be.

Because when you see things from and through the eyes of love, you will see that everyone is guiding you back to yourself, to love, you will see that fear is guiding you to love. Every single thing whether it is perceived as bad or good is guiding you to love.

And you have chosen these experiences. By accepting this as if you have chosen it, is the moment you come from love and not fear.

In the grand scheme of the infinite this here is just a small experience, a moment. You might as well just enjoy this experience of creation and love.

Why are you worried? You have done this a million times. Know that all you see is your perspectives when you look out into the world.

....

....

Let's begin

Through these words and as we speak, a vibration will be integrated so as to assist you with releasing all the matters we have decided to speak about today.

So we will begin to say that in order for us to continue to change we need to change our parenting style, as it is in our youth that the future lies.

So, when we judge our children through anger, we are not only belittling them but making them feel less than.

70

And this leads to resentment because of the anger and judgement from the parent.

Any form of judgement is going to end in resentment, because what judgement is, is someone pushing what they believe or what they prefer onto another, instead of allowing the person to be and feel as they do, without restriction or limitation.

Perhaps to the child what they did was not wrong, but to you it is wrong. But what this causes is a separation within the child, where the mind and soul does not agree.

If this goes on long enough it can cause a conflict within the child or person, it can eventually cause dementia, Alzheimer's, bipolar or psychotic breaks.

The best thing to do is to ask yourself "what would God do in this moment?", "what would love do?"

How would I have wanted to be parented?

And then from that standpoint act accordingly.

When a child does something that feels immorally incorrect to them, this already creates shame within them.

Guilt is something that people put on you when they recognize your shame.

So, a child does something that you feel is incorrect and you punish them with anger, it is not only going to create conflict within the parent-child relationship but conflict within the child. There will be conflict within the child's own guidance system, their truth and the mind.

Allow children to discover and uncover their own versions of right and wrong and their own versions of truth.

Allow them to discover themselves and choose how they want the world to look. Allow them to fully express their interests and inner desires because if you don't, suppression within the child might follow.

Now we will move onto fear or evil....

Evil is for some people something unseen, it's the demon, it's the rape and murder, it's the nightmare, and it's the possession.

It's because of this fear that we allow things to hold power over us. When really, we look at them and we see this is just an energy that wants to be loved. People come to Riana all the time saying that they are cursed and evil and when she looks at them all she sees is deep unprocessed sadness.

All it is, was just sadness.

Generally, anger is associated with evil. Evil is caused by suppressed anger—anger that has been accumulating since childhood. For example, when a 3-year-old is not allowed to be angry, and is forced to suppress their anger, and so it builds up so much that eventually it needs an outlet.

When the anger is finally released, it is often comes in the form of violence, including rape, murder, and many other abuses in later years.

And it all stemmed from a perceived version that what they were feeling was bad.

We need to go back to the root. We need to go back to the root. The murderer is often just a child who wanted to be understood when he was three years old. That chain reaction led him to kill someone. The murderer, the rapist, the misogynist, is just a child whose emotional needs were never met. And now he is an adult trying to function as an adult but really, he is a child screaming out in pain.

So, let's make an example, your partner comes home and is triggered by you, and he is angry, which is also a sign of suppressed anger by the way. Now what would happen instead of you reacting angrily back, what if you just hugged him?

As much as he would try and resist it, that hug will have made him feel good somehow.

They might push you away but it's going to change them, it's going to change them. Because if in their darkest moment you can come at them with utmost love and compassion, they are going to shift. And when they shift, they might think: "I am worth that loving response." So, if anyone in your life is angry and has those moments of rage, the best thing you can do is just give them the most compassionate hug. Just hold them. Go in with that deep feeling of love.

And if that causes you fear then let it go, because that is the cure.

Love is the Cure.

You're in their life for a reason. In an abusive relationship the husband verbally abuses the wife. But for some reason the person being abused generally stays in the relationship.

Why? There is divine reason for that.

If you are staying it is because you care for them and you know it's not really them.

Spirit is saying Riana don't be nice today.

So, if you are in a relationship like that, you have chosen to be in that relationship. Not only that, you are a vibrational match to this person. Meaning that he will mirror things in you that needs attention and vice versa. You can't be passive about it anymore. You have been attracted together because of your passiveness. They are not only going to challenge your passiveness and help you to grow but you are going to help them too. And you can do that by first standing up with your truth and then coming in with that deep compassionate love. And say I love you...I love you so much, maybe it's not a deep romantic love but it's a love that carries on because you know deep in your heart that they are an expression of you. And that by helping them you are helping yourself too. By helping yourself, you are helping them too. Let's just take a second here and exhale, spirit is saying let's just allow that out now....

Breathe it out right now

All we have in this life most obviously is the relationships, the connections. We have been given all of these different guides who are interchangeably the same as us. In an alternative life we are them. They are us. And when you really think about it, this stranger is actually me and in a different reality I am them. So, if you back out of a relationship and say this relationship is too hard too difficult, or you don't like it then you are coming from some sort of fear. Then you are destined to play the same scenario over and over again through other relationships. Until you understand, heal and learn from it. You will just see a different face, but same issue.

Time does not exist. Time will contract and expand until you have learnt the lesson.

We must let these toxic emotions go, all these old perspectives go, and learn all the lessons that our soul requires. But if you rather look at your current relationships and see what it is that it is trying to teach you, all of a sudden things improve in the relationship or the relationship just ends and you part ways having learned and healed and raised to a new higher vibration. You have completed the lesson out of love instead of fear and now you have no attachment to it. Fear has attachment, Love does not.

Then you get to that point you see every reflection of yourself in every single person that you meet.

Make every single person your guide, your best friend in being your teacher.

Recently what I have noticed is that the timelines have opened meaning that one can now learn all your lessons in a week, you could learn all your lessons tomorrow if you wanted to. Your biggest lessons will always be very apparent in your life. What did you come to learn, lack, scarcity, rage, fear etc.

When you learn those prominent ones to the best of your ability you will be free to create whatever you want. Also living much much longer as of now.

Close your eyes now,

Get comfortable. Start to breathe deeply in through the nose into the belly.

Hold for 5 seconds and then slowly exhale through the mouth.

Do this now to get into a meditative state as spirit begins to channel and clear all the old.

Do this now for about a minute and then come back and continue reading……

Let's Begin with the activation and clearing now

Hello….

We are coming in as the Divine Collective,

We are all coming in collectively here all in one consciousness now, as usual.

Alright so we are moving into a portal or gateway now, releasing meditation.

Feel us fill the room

Whichever room you are in, feel us gather with you

Feel us in the room that you are in now.

Perhaps some of you will feel the ocean coming in as you are surrounded by water. Filling your room up with beautiful crystal-clear ocean water. Perhaps creating a vortex now somewhere in your house.

As you see the water rise you can see that the vortex is apparent in one area. Right now, the vortex is directly above this book but yours can be wherever you intuitively feel it is.

We are sending you symbols now, many of you may receive them.... just relaxing

The more centred you are the easier these symbols will be to perceive and receive.

Some of you may be getting downloads of information, akashic records you may call it.

Remembering, connecting, numbers, sequences, sacred geometry symbols, all of it is being given and downloaded to you, now.

Knowing that every single person here reading this, yes even you! Is an energy transmitter and transmuter. You are not only giving out energy but energy that is transmuted to you is transmuted instantly to love and light, knowing that there is absolutely no energy that exists that is not yours. And then that statement alone can allow fear to dissipate…. now.

You may see that now your room has become full of water. Perhaps you're in the water and notice that you can breathe. Quite easily, water is an instant transmuter, cleanser and purifier. Detoxifier.

Breathe it in.

You are breathing just fine you see

We are here, look around.

You may notice some of us, all of us.

You might recognize us, you might feel us.

You might sense us; you might know we are there. Either way, we are.

And thank you for allowing us in.

Every single one of us comes in peace, every single one.

The biggest fear you have in your life – perhaps we are showing you now. We will show you one example.

You fear what you cannot see, many of you, most of you. You fear the dark, you fear what you do not know. We promise you the dark and what you do not know is a perception, is a limited belief.

Perhaps you fear the terrorist. You have heard about on TV; you fear him or her.

That's about as real as fear is, okay. That is the most fear that can be had. If you fear the dark or the unknown more than you fear serial killer or rapist, or the terrorist then you are being highly delusional.

What you have here in your 3d reality is much more real than the vibration of evil than anything else outside of what you cannot understand.

There is no such thing as an evil spirit.

No such thing.

There's no such thing as a spell or a curse, there's no such thing as darkness holding you down because there is no such thing as darkness.

So, if you can get past the fear of a serial killer or the fear of a terrorist, then you can get passed anything and everything.

Just like we said earlier, the serial killer, the murderer, all he wanted to be was to be heard when he was 3 years old. He just wanted to feel understood. He is not evil; he was born pure as day as all of you are. He just simply perceives things that way. And in his true essence when he wakes up in the morning. He is sad. He does not want to feel this way anymore, he is lost he is confused. Because underneath all of the fear is love. It's always been there, and it will always be there.

When a soul sheds their physical body, the vessel that allows them to experience and move in 3d, when they shed their mind, a part of them that allows them to perceive things linearly (In a line), when it sheds that, it goes back into its form of love. Just like how every single one of who has awoken to the truth that you are all one, all you wanted to do was to experience more and more love. That's because that's all there is.

There is no such thing as a person who is evil. And you know this, because there is no such thing as an evil baby.

Perhaps the baby when it was born took on some of the frequencies of the mother and father. But the baby is not evil nor is anything. Every single one of you here in the essence of how expanded your
78

consciousness truly is, is just a small child, in a scale of awareness. And even with that small small scale, one percent out of a million hundred thousand, that one percent of awareness that you do have…. choose love.

Could you imagine if it was a 100 percent or a 1000 percent. That's why your physical plane is the only plane in the entire universe that experiences these perceptions that there is not only love. There are similar planes as yours, going through very similar things, and we just see it as a child learning to ride their bike, it is no more than that. It does not fear us for we do not experience fear.

We enjoy watching you learn; it gives us and brings us great joy. We are now here to help you to remember, to assist you in remembering. There has never been anything, anything outside of yourself that is hindering you, everything that you perceive around you is a reflection and projection of what is going on within you. It's so simple.

Like we said there is absolutely nothing that does not exist within you. So, when you hear about that murderer on the TV you do not go and hide in the basement, you go within and you see where this is coming from. Where is this projection coming from? What part of me has this within me, where can I let it go? And then you do.

So, we are now going to be triggering some fear. If you feel you are ready, we are going to be triggering some fear within you.

Know that there is no way to get hurt. This is only for joy. Because that is what you are.

So, you may feel the fear arise.

You may feel it coming in all senses.

Just let it come. Just surrender and trust us.

Trust us as you.

Trust us as God.

For all of us together, we form God in all its glory of love.

And as we said we are interchangeably the same.

All connected, on a level that you are not yet aware of.

So, allow the fear to arise.

Whatever is hidden within you is coming up. Now

Maybe you feel pains. Maybe you feel the energy coming in.

Different areas could be cold or warm.

Maybe you feel emotional.

Maybe you have a bad taste in your mouth, or you smell a bad smell.

A funny smell we should say.

Maybe your thoughts are going sideways, you just going to allow it to come.

We could use the word consume, because we know that triggers. Trust us.

It's okay let it go.

Let it come.

Smile

Surrender

Trust

You are love that's all you have ever been.

As soon as you trust that that's who you are, you let go.

Feel it coming up, arising within you now.

Pains, fears, triggers all forming.

But you smile

All the creation of your suppression of truth.

Now holding space, there is no way to do this wrong. We are assisting you

Remember that you are completely safe.

We going to hold space as you smile.

You're striving to create a neutral vibration.

Feel it and know it. Knowing that this neutral vibration is love.

Love is unlabeled. When you un-label something you allow it to be released.

Surrendering to this neutral vibration of love.

As you breathe naturally with your feet on the floor. Knowing that there is no way to do this wrong.

The entire body might start to tingle as you accept and feel lightness flowing in through your feet.

All the information earlier is coming to great use. You are able to access it an acknowledge it and let these feelings and limited perspectives go. Allowing the triggers to come, observing them from the highest perspective, from the outside in. For through this information. lessons can and has been heard and learnt and integrated. And now you continue to release fear.

Looking at the big picture and observing these feelings arise. All perceived fear.

Feel doubt arise. Know that that is a limited belief. You know you are doing this. You are being love.

Feel all your pain.

Repeating now, I am open......I am open

I am open

Feel how open you are

You can raise your head up

Pause

Pause

Pause

You may see versions of your old self, panicking, freaking out.

You are just going to let them go.

And you may even see yourself dying, ceasing to breathe.

Let that go.

Your breath becoming empowered, as even the air that you breathe vibrates at the frequency of love.

Now again letting go of the fear that you are doing it wrong.

Or the fear that something may be trapped. Letting go of all those fears.

82

Letting go of the fear that something will stay within you. We say to you now….

The floodgates have been opened, for massive healing.

Nothing is outside of yourself, remember that.

Let it go.

If you feel any kind of reaction to things in the past, continue to let them go. We are with you.

If you feel you are up for the challenge, you can put this book down and turn down the lights. For many people fear started in the dark.

We are now going to release it as a limiting belief. Take a moment now. Turn off the lights.

Now sitting in the darkness, allow it to bring up all the rest. You may get a little bit nauseous, and that's okay because we are going to release the physical now.

All of the fears you may have forgotten about or overlooked. If you feel something is not leaving you can say, "it's okay you can stay. If you need to stay you can stay".

You are giving it compassion and love. And just by doing this it most likely will be able to be released.

Do this now, and know, sense, see or feel it being released.

Come back to this book in a few minutes.

Welcome back.

Now envisioning yourself as the world, seeing every single person as you.

Surrounding your body now with love, as you are sitting there bathed in this beautiful water. Seeing all the people on earth as you care for them and love them. Only see why they are hurt and why they hurt. Love others as if it is your own child.

You are looking at the big picture now, how simple it is, just to let go and trust that love is all there is. Period.

Feel your crown awakening and your third eye pulse, as all the beings of love surround you in awe at your beauty and your service. Every single one of you are amazing. All the beings around you now clapping and cheering for you, coming up to you now to give you a big hug, as you float in this glorious pool of water, this holy infused water. You feel the compassion in every one of us as you, as the love you have for your child, as God is, as you are.

It is done.

We are here once again to applaud you in your generous, glorious and honourable acts. Your service to divinity and to the collective is more appreciated than you will ever understand. Your work here not only strengthens you but all of us as one. You have rid dis-ease today and you will continue to release as we support you as you continue this book and continue this journey. As you begin to master the techniques and teachings in this book you will begin to expand more and more as love.

You will receive the rewards tenfold; we promise you.

Every single one of you will be rewarded. There are many of you now who has had a sudden awakening, some of you who is experiencing bliss and light, and that is amazing. For those of you who may feel a little bit less than that know that you are safe and secure. As we said nothing can hurt you because all there is, is love. It doesn't matter what you are perceiving right now, you are letting it go.

Say this to yourself silently now: I love you

I love all parts of you. Looking within as you say this...

I love you

Thank you, thank you

Thank You

Your fear of an unfinished process may keep your fear unprocessed, although there is no finished line. Let go now of that fear of unfinished business.

Be grateful for how you feel right now.

That is, it!

The acceptance, there is no more denial. The accepting of that that is, is all you need to clear it.

The accepting that you might not do it all now, will increase its release time tenfold.

Accepting.

Feeling that warmth coming over you.

As you feel accepting, and how you feel right now whichever way it is, feel how strong your breathe is right now. How much you can breathe compared to before this.

Repeating this now, I am perfect right now....

I am perfect right now

I am perfect right now

I accept me as…. I AM

I AM THAT I AM

I AM THAT I AM

Bearing down now and accepting it.

Knowing that not accepting it is fear and allowing it to stay.

Holding space, opening the channel to allow anything that's ready to just go.

Feeling the vibration in your bones, in your skin, in your aura

As you let go.

And so, it is.

You have now reached and scraped the bottom of the barrel and now ready to continue with the teachings to follow in this Book. Teachings that will allow you to master the art of you and the art of transmuting all that doesn't serve you.

You are Divine

Take a moment now before moving on to the next part.

The Revelation

During my 3 years of isolation and intensive self-healing I accessed higher states of consciousness and unbeknownst to me, I would return back into my body with Source blueprints from the highest realms of creation that would one day serve as the Ascension Blueprint for those on the Awakening Path - known as The Seraphim Order. After a series of supernatural and synchronistic events, I was shown where my soul originates from and then, shortly after this during a meditation, I was approached and commissioned by the Mighty Order of the Seraphim, and began the process of merging my consciousness with my consciousness as part of the Seraphim council and further mentor with them to bring The Seraphim Wisdom, Order and Initiations to the world as a Master Creator Teacher and Sage. And this was when the entirety of The Seraphim Order was birthed - which consists of 6 Source Codes of initiation in embodying your true divine self. I have heard the term Seraphim at this point, but I did not know exactly who they were and what purpose they held. And by accessing my consciousness as part of the Seraphim council, I received telepathic knowledge of my now mission, and who the Seraphim are and what their purpose to humanity is.

Who Are The Seraphim Angels

The Seraphim were designed as the Mightiest beings ever created within the universe. They are the direct feminine emanation of God Source and are known as the highest order of the Angels.They are a lineage within the highest angelic order who attends to the throne and light of Source, from which all of creation is birthed and created. They are responsible for birthing creations and now they assist humanity and those who are ready to embody their true essence, in activating our embodiment as Creators. Their message to us is that we have all been designed to create as Source creates, for the light of Source is within us all. The Seraphim reminds us that as angelic beings they too have free will, however they choose to consecrate their free will to the divine will of Source within. They are responsible for having birthed new worlds, species and universes since the beginning of time. The

Seraphim are known to initiate and ordain beings into their own Self Mastery and Embodiment of their Divinity as Creators.

They appear to humanity now as guides to initiate us into the next golden age. They only usually step forward and make themselves visible when humanity reaches or graduates to a certain point of evolution. And now they bring their mighty power and wisdom forth and are ready to assist us in our sovereign embodiment.

The Seraphim appear in this cosmology as some of the highest ascended teachers available for mentoring us in how to actually embody our sovereign divine nature within human form. They are the collective consciousness that assist in governing the universe and galaxies that is in the Divine order of the Universal alignment and flow.

The Seraphim Source System which is being brought forth now, is designed to activate your unlimited potential as a Sovereign Creator.

Seraphim Wisdom and Healing

The Seraphim introduces an advanced spiritual system that has been dormant for thousands of years. Thirteen thousand years ago The Seraphim created a cosmology of initiations and codes. The Seraphim taught these ancient codes during a golden age thousands of years ago, in mystery schools, initiating masters and teachers to their full embodiment as creators activating their individual gifts and superpowers. The Seraphim are known to ordain any being before graduating as an Ascended Master.

The Seraphim Order

Through mentoring with the Mighty Seraphim, we have now completed Humanities Ascension Blueprint for Healing, called the Seraphim Order TM. It is designed to assist all those who are awake to begin to and furthermore rapidly expand into the embodiment of their Higher Selves. This Book, You Are The Creator serves as an introduction to the Spiritual Journey and Spiritual Healing Process, being mentored and guided by the Angels, the Ascended Masters and other Cosmic guides. The Seraphim Order will be an online programme, consisting of 6 Source Code Initiations, which I believe is the Ascension Blueprint for true and complete embodiment of all your lives of Mastery, allowing you to truly step into your power and purpose as the Creator.

The Seraphim Order Series will be available shortly after the publication of this book.

CHAPTER 3:

Everything Aims to Awaken You

You are always being guided...

Dare you even entertain, much less welcome, embrace and put into action your highest dreams and visions about what life, love and who we should be? Well I tell you this today, if you dare to dream it, it must be yours. And this book will show you that it is possible.

Your life, as it were, have all been perfectly designed and created by the most omnipotent creator of all that is: God/Source/Universe/The Divine embodied as You. And you are being guided each and every moment.

You are always guided

Each and every person has a team of light beings assigned to them to guide them on their journey to a higher path. These will consist of passed loved ones, our higher angelic realm, spirit guides, and god energy. If you open yourselves up to the secret language of your spiritual team your life will transform in the most profound ways. Here's another truth, the universe has been conspiring to help us long before our soul's arrival on this earth. Our teams have long been in place. It is now our responsibility to open up to these divine messages of guidance awaiting us. You are being guided every single day of your life, there is most certainly a divine force walking beside you, as they are with me, asking you to consciously create your reality and live life intuitively, all you must do is turn the switch on and align with your higher self. The Divine Universe has many ways that it sends you messages, some are signs and synchronicities, and others are lessons and experiences. Our job is to stay present and focused in the here and now, staying mindful and attuned to our intuitive senses. It can be can be a little difficult at first to decipher and learn to read the signs, not because they are not clear, but because your ego will get in the way until you teach yourself to trust, allow, and perceive life in a different way. It's a bit like looking in your peripheral vision, instead of straight ahead like you have always conditioned to do.

Signs and Messages are different for everyone; the Divine Universe brings the ones that you need specifically for you and your life. Believe that there is more to life than "this" and you will begin to see more.

Spirit would like to intervene here, "We would like to take the opportunity now to attune you to a higher vibration, so as to be open to seeing these messages and signs in your daily life. Dear one all you need to do is say, "Yes, I am open to receiving now" and you will be attuned."

Take a moment dear one and say this now, should you choose this attunement of the divine.

Pause to sit in silence and affirm this yes.

Now I will continue to describe the different types of signs and messages that the divine/ the universe sends you…to guide and let you know that you are not alone.

Synchronicities

One of my favourites, this can also be called divine time and divine intervention; a moment of your existence that you are brought exactly what you need right when you need it. The Divine Universe lines up the experiences and the signs you require to show you the way. Have you ever thought about someone and then bumped into them or received a call from them on the same day or even minutes later? Perhaps you have happened upon a chance meeting or coincidence that has brought you a certain answer. You have been in the right place, right time at least once in your life, this is the power of Divine synchronicity and time. You could be feeling down and you ask for a sign as to what you can do to heal and later you're out and about and you just happen to hear a conversation between strangers about a great book they read regarding healing, you catch the title and can go and buy it now. Synchronicity is a powerful revelation and indication that you are on the right path and whatever is happening is for your highest good. You don't just happen upon something, someone or an experience by chance, and if you catch yourself saying "what a coincidence" or "this seems like it was meant for me" then you know you are being guided by a Universal force. You must be aware of synchronicities, don't dismiss anything that catches your attention and resonates with what you have been needing, asking for, or seeking direction on. There is no such thing as coincidence, period.

Stopped/Blocked or Delayed

I know if I am blocked from moving forward it is for good reason, I must either adjust or re-evaluate my plan, or, I there's a lesson inherent in the situation at hand. When I hit a blockade, I always re-evaluate and then proceed. The same goes for delays, the Divine Universe doesn't want to hinder your progress, but what's best for you according to your limited perspective, isn't always what you think it is. Delaying you is a blessing in disguise and often the delay brings you to what you needed in the first place. Sometimes delays can even save your life. Whenever I am stuck in traffic or stuck for some reason, I always tell myself I must be being protected from something and redirected for my betterment.

Being stopped is a big one too, and you should truly acknowledge when you are shown to do so; the "stop" can be a deep feeling you have or a warning sign you have been given, you may even experience a complete stop in what you're doing. Trust in the process, everything happens for a reason. Look to these moments as blessings in disguise, if you can raise your perception and see a bigger picture the blessings

92

become clearer. A stop is also an indication that you may be off track or, a certain person or situation isn't what is best for you. In these moments, I usually find myself being taken down a new path. Blessings in Disguise – through one's external reality

I discussed a bit when it came to being stopped, blocked and delayed, but there is more to your blessings in disguise. Sometimes life happens and drastically alters your course of direction, what you once knew and held a comfort zone in is no longer, and you probably have been launched from your safety and comfortableness (or what you believed was safe and comfortable) into the big wide open space of "what the heck just happened" I have had many of these blessings happen to me, most of them ripped my whole world apart, and at the time I thought it was the end of life as I knew it. I can now look back and see it was the beginning to a rebirth or transformation for me.

Especially as you begin to heal, your vibration or frequency will change, and this means you might not be a match to certain people, places, environments, jobs and situations anymore. You will either no longer resonate with them or the law of attraction will be in action based on your new vibration and beliefs. It was so prevalent for me when I lost my job, I realized that I was no longer a match to that job and people anymore, and the universe provided me another job which would further allow me the opportunity to increase my vibration and awareness.

Don't ever take the hurdles and alterations at face value, if life is being torn down, it is probably because it needs to be rebuilt. A blessing in disguise has no hard or easy way, it just is. Life is eternal, and through our hardships and our losses, we can begin to appreciate the beauty of divine timing and divine intervention. You may not always like them, but they are what they are, a blessing that changes your life in a very significant way. Trust It.

Then there are also various signs and symbolisms, the Divine Universe send to you…

From numbers to animals and even insects. The thing about signs is that they are everyday "ordinary" things that can pass you by if you keep looking at them as ordinary. A sign is something that calls to our intuition as having special significance or meaning to us in that moment or time in our life where we require guidance. Signs need your awareness and attention. If you're going to ask for a sign, then you must be willing to be present throughout your entire day. Be specific, if you want to know if you will move, ask for a white cat to cross your path, this cat can come in an image, an actual cat, or however it needs to be shown to you. If you ask, you shall receive.

Angel Numbers

Angel Numbers are one way you receive signs; 1111, 1212, 888, 234 are just a few sequences you can see. Repetitive numbers are also significant and are strong messages you should acknowledge. Numbers will catch your attention, especially if you are seeing them often, you should become aware of how numbers cross your path.

Most people who begin their spiritual awakening see the number 1111, you might see it on the clock, license plates and even your grocery receipt. This number is sent to remind you of your power to manifest your thoughts into reality, so you should re-evaluate and make sure that your thoughts are in a positive frame of creation. This sign has kept me from falling into a trap of negativity which certain events in my life may carry.

Animals

We are certain to cross the path of a mighty animal at some point in our lives, and we always cross the path of our everyday animals, but did you know they can have a message for you every day. For the mighty animals like the Bear, Wolf, Tiger etc., they cross your path a

94

little less frequently; when they do though, you are to acknowledge their spirit message.

A spirit animal can come to you in a dream, a picture or image you see, and in real life. You will know if the animal has a message for you because you will feel it.

Birds like owls, hawks, eagles, crows, chickadees, hummingbirds etc. Cross your path more frequent, but their message changes each time you see them. Messages will be very intuitive and based on where you are in life. These animals are either a Messenger, or your Spirit animal.

Insects

They carry messages, some of you may just laugh at this notion because it's a silly insect that is nothing special. Every single insect carries a divine message for you. They are divine messengers, spirit guides and even shadow spirit guides, wanting to guide and assist you on your path.

Butterflies, Dragonflies, Moths and Ladybugs are carriers of divine light, they often will linger or hover around you when the divine wants to connect. It is also a sign your loved ones passed are near. When any insect acts strange and seems to be catching your attention out of the ordinary, know that you are on the right path and in sync with the spirit world.

Feathers

They can appear in the oddest places, I once found one in my house on numerous occasions. It doesn't matter how they get there, what matters is they crossed your path and each colour has its own message.

Quotes

Those ones you come across more than once in a matter of a few days. Sayings that speak to you and appear when you need that extra boost. Pay attention to those little messages that come into your line of sight, they are made just for you.

Music

A song that happens to come on the radio at the perfect time, or "happens" to play at significant moments in your life, is a divine message for you. Music can help heal, it can bring up hidden emotions; play on your heart; make you feel joy, and it happens to be a powerful vibration that triggers your emotions and intuition. There are also those songs that come on that seem to answer you, like if you ask if you are on the right path and a song plays that makes you "know" you are. Music plays for you, have some fun with it and listen to the messages that are brought to you. Sometimes I ask what I need to know be brought to me in the next song that plays on the radio. It always brings me a profound message when I do this. There were moments I can remember when I would wake up with a song in my head and I hadn't heard that song in a long time, I actually sometimes don't even recall knowing the song, but yet the songs melody and few words were repeatedly playing over and over in my head. Immediately I would go to my computer and browse the songs words, and there would always be a fitting message from the divine/my higher self.

Dreams

The divine universe uses your dreams as a direct way to communicate to your subconscious. You can learn to interpret your dreams by remembering everything you can about them. Meditations also helps you to open up or access your subconscious which will help with lucid dreaming. Some dreams you will recall everything, and some you will only remember bits and pieces. Others you may not recall anything, but you will wake up with a feeling that something happened while you were asleep. It is important to get a good night's sleep and make the intention to dream. We all dream, just because you don't remember doesn't mean it didn't happen.

Intuition

Obviously, this is the number one way of divine communication, what you see, hear, feel and think within your higher self and your consciousness of connection. Your intuition is your inner compass and guide which the universe is always fully connected with. Learning to trust your inner voice and "knowing", listen to the messages you hear or sense within you that seem to be connected to something bigger than you. Your intuition is usually your first gut instinct or your first thought.

You are always guided and supported by the Divine Universe, begin to be open to divine guidance and become aware of your connection.

The shadow self is the portal to your divine power

That one problem that just never seems to go away, creeps up on us in different forms with different faces. The one problem we can never seem to fix in order to get to the other side. This mysterious sacred problem is the very thing calling you into your expansion - that calls you into liberation. Only when we have fully seen this aspect as not an enemy but an ally, embraced, surrendered, danced with, softened and sensed into it fully, allowing it to shape us and break us open, becoming completely naked with it – will we experience the revelation. Allow your hearts to be torn apart, integrating both dark and light. It is a necessary and important component along this spiritual alchemic journey towards liberation – this is how your power begins to fully express itself through you.

Riana Arendse

Many believe their shadow, or darker side, is the enemy. This mindset is very detrimental. We push these fearful, wounded parts of ourselves away, instead of welcoming that part who is you, back into wholeness. These parts are worthy of being loved, as they are a part of you.

But usually they are parts of you that have fractured off during traumatic times, when the emotional hurt could not have been worked through and released. Instead it sits there as a wounded child who we reject over and over again.

This SHADOW aspect is out to awaken us every single moment.

This SHADOW aspect is the direct link to integrating our Highest Selves.

The Shadow side is the aspect of us that our inherent purpose lies.

Want to know your purpose?

Face your shadow, you will find it there.

The shadow side is the Gift, the teacher, the guide and the hidden pot of Gold at the end of the rainbow. The shadow is not a problem that needs a solution, in fact it is the solution. Beneath the soil that which is our shadow aspects, lies rich beautiful soil and seeds that will open up our potentiality in ways we cannot imagine. Facing and integrating the shadow side will birth a new reality that will alter your view of self and the world. Embracing this part of ourselves, our fears, our anxieties our disassociated personas, will urge us to move more

98

fearlessly and powerfully towards our highest potential. It will bring us back into wholeness again, to retrieve and claim our power back.

Where is the shadow self-more evident in our lives?

We see our shadow in everything, in our encounters with others, our mirrors and in our behaviors. Our shadow lies hidden beneath the subconscious mind, but eventually winds up taking control over us and our lives. In essence, we end up with a traumatized 3-year-old child running our lives. Our shadow rouses us to act out in ways we never imagined, and can result in bad habits, acting out, addictions, self-sabotage and repetitive negative behaviors. Our shadow keeps us from living our full potentiality, speaking our truth and living an authentic life. But what we tend to do when the shadow aspect makes itself known is, we tend to run or hide. Suppressing this aspect is an action based on fear. But what one doesn't know is that doing this only give it more power over us, resulting in more pain, more suffering and more fear.

All of this begs some questions we must consider.

Why do we have access to so much wisdom when we awaken, and yet fail to integrate this truth and knowing into our reality?

Why are we unable to fully sustain being present in the now, and always get triggered?

Why does it remain so difficult for us to act according to our inner values and not past conditions?

It is because of our Shadow Self that all our power lies hidden. And right here is where we will find the key to liberation and healing.

The first move in beginning to come back into wholeness is to accept duality as a part of ourselves. Duality meaning both dark and light or negative and positive. This is what humanity struggles with, this is what causes suffering. Duality, life and death, good and evil, dark and light all coexists in every single person and makes itself manifest in every part of our lives. One cannot experience our god selves without experiencing the opposite. One cannot experience love without having to experience fear, and yet most of us ignore or deny our dualistic nature. The first step therefore in Self Mastery is going inward and reconnecting with that innate force, hidden within our shadow aspect.

We will delve more into the Shadow aspect in later chapters when we begin the work of Un-becoming.

CHAPTER 4:

The Art of Surrender

An opportunity to surrender – allowing

"The ultimate result of all suffering in the world is that it will force humans into realizing who they are beyond the separate sense of self. What we perceive as suffering from our limited perspective is actually part of a greater higher perspective of consciousness. We are far more than this body, we are part of a unified stream, out of which all these limited and fleeting forms emerge, and to which they will return."-

Riana Arendse

Some spiritual teachers believe that one needs to detach completely from all one's desires, however we cannot un-desire a desire. It is not the desire that causes suffering but one's attachment to the desire. You can still desire, manifest this desire into creation without being detached from all of life completely.

Your suffering is only found within your story, the mind-made story. When you're aligned within the present moment, you'll be able to access enormous power. Things such as anxiety, stress and negativity limit your ability to access that inherent power. As these emotions are only present when we are attached to the formless and to the stories we tell ourselves, that which is temporary and passing.

When you are anxious, you are experiencing Fear -you are experiencing too much attachment to your mind and thoughts, then being Present in the here and now. Anxiety is a future-directed psychological fear of something that might happen. However, the Future is always Imagined and Always Illusory. Anxiety only gets worse when we are in a state of Resistance, yet we resist it in order to stop the anxious feelings from occurring, but all it does is make things worse. By focusing on what you don't want, you attract more of it – this indeed is the law of attraction.

Overcoming anxiety

To be liberated from anxiety you must surrender to it completely. You must completely release the resistance and be present, completely present, with the anxiety itself and surrender to what is. This requires being in a state of awareness in which you can observe the thoughts that create the anxious feelings. When you become aware of the thoughts, you will realize that you are not your thoughts, and that they are merely an illusionary idea of yourself.

A very strange thing can occur at exactly the point you realize there is no escaping the imaginary world of your illusions. It happens when you bare your heart open to illusion, surrender your eternal struggle against it, and admit to being bound by it. That is when transformation occurs. You can never be anything you are consciously aware of, for these thoughts are only appearances within your consciousness. Let go of your attachment to solution and resolution and accept what is right here and right now—without resistance.

The solution comes when we realize there is no problem at all. There never was. It is all simply resistance.

Go deep within, be still, and be passively watchful. Be patient, be self-loving. When you realize your anxiety and illusory thoughts—the whole thing—are a fiction of your mind, you will start to see what is true and experience the greatest freedom. Then you will be free from the kind of suffering that comes from the false belief that something is always happening to you, or that you have "personal problems," or that you are lacking this or that, or that you have somehow been wronged by the world, by life itself. Soon you will discover that your suffering is confined to the story you have written in your mind. No story, no more suffering.

In truth, all happenings appear for you. Every perceivable moment that arises within your life is an opportunity for you to awaken, to transcend your humanity, and to realize your *Self* as Awareness.

Merge your awareness into the anxiety itself - BECOME the anxiety, rather than its experiencer. Become the actual energetic vibration which is perceived.

Realize that you are not separate from it, you are it.

Be Present in the now moment and see the truth of what this is and who you are.

When one gets to a later stage during the spiritual awakening journey, we get to a point of completely transcending self or ego. And towards the end of this stage, it feels as if nothing can save you, it feels like you have completely failed, being stripped away of all your beliefs, opinions, stories, personas and identities.

Nothing to hold onto anymore. It could feel as if you have failed miserably. The "great death" of self will feel like death.

But this feeling of failing, of death, is a key step. Why? Because it allows the ego (that falsely believes "success" is a win-lose proposition) to completely die off. Once the ego is out of the equation (and can no longer manipulate ideas, concepts, or tangibles), it won't be able to hold us captive to fear of failing. Only then will we come to realize that the whole "failure and success" thing is really just an illusion, merely something we came to falsely believe.

Imagine reaching a point where becoming someone or something—defining yourself by worldly failure or success—is meaningless and no longer holds you hostage. Imagine fully knowing you are a powerful being, inherent with divine love, and the creator of your own reality. Imagine reaching the absolute realization that you are more than just the constructs of our mind, and your attachments.......Imagine coming to the absolute realization of who this really is, that is standing in our shoes and peering through our eyes.

Do you feel that?

Do you feel that inner knowing and remembrance, that sense of liberation?

....

There are two kinds of suffering: one that leads to more suffering and one that leads to dissolution of suffering. Only true surrender leads to dissolution of suffering and true freedom.

This journey of awakening and enlightenment brings about this realization - (great doubt, great surrender, and great death) and then ultimately the embodiment and expression of this realization.

So, starting right now, in this moment, I am asking you to become Source/God/the Divine. I am asking you to take your stand, to stand absolutely firm in your intention to awaken to the truth of your *self*.

The power of this very simple, yet unwavering intention and absolute stand to be liberated in this lifetime can propel you to awaken to the simple fact that you and all beings are liberated.

At each and every moment from here on out, have the intention to directly experience Truth, as it truly is.

Don't think about the Truth or what it could be —directly return to your experience here, now, moment to moment.

Be Present.

When one finds that in order to realize and embody ultimate happiness, one must surrender, one begins to ask, "How happy can I possibly be without control of my life? Without control of my journey? Without control of my destination, forced out of the driver's seat and into the passenger's seat?" But those questions stem from the ego, from a state of separation.

Instead, we must realize that we are the passenger, the driver, the vehicle, life, the journey, and the destination itself—that we are, in fact, consciousness itself. In reality, in all truth, consciousness is what we are. So, surrendering means to let go and allow our highest truths, highest potentials, and highest possibilities to come forth.

"It is important to understand we cannot perceive or even grasp this idea from the state of separate self, from the perception of our minds. That's why it takes a great level of trust and surrender to realize and embody our true inner essence and watch it unfold before our eyes.

Giving up vs Surrender

There is no other step on the journey that happens as instantaneously as Surrender; but, it may take a very long time until we are ready to fully do so. When we do, our prior step of searching usually moves towards its end. Nearly simultaneously, the next step after Surrender - healing - begins. As we move deeper into the soul level of the journey,

Let me make it clear that surrendering and giving up are not the same thing. Instead, we first give up in order to surrender. We are simply exhausted. Unable to solve our problems or find answers, we throw up our hands in defeat.

Once we give up, the opportunity is there for us to discover a higher power that is always available to assist us. Not everyone surrenders, and if they simply give up and end things there, the spiritual journey may come to an end. For those who do move into that instant realization of Surrender, rather than feeling defeated we are flooded with an enormous sense of relief and hope.

Fear is why we do not surrender. The egoic self- identity is based in fear. Our attachment to it and its survival is why we do not truly awaken. We may experience moments of freedom, as many spiritual teachers have, but then the fear returns and we "play it safe." We seek a balance between being awake and being asleep. It sounds good to the ego, but this balance is an illusion. This balance does not exist. We either fully surrender the illusion or we don't.

The key to true surrender is to surrender permanently; not a temporary surrender to achieve a specific thing, person, or situation, but a complete surrender of your life and everything you have ever come to know. "Letting go and surrendering" is truly the secret of spiritual awakening.

CHAPTER 5:

Get Divinely Aligned First

The necessity of looking inward

To actualize healing, inner wealth, outer wealth, or alignment with source, we must look inward first. Therefore, you must acknowledge the role your "energy field" plays in the creation of your experiences.

Begin by: 1) evaluating all aspects of your consciousness that affect your energy field, including your most repetitive thoughts, emotions, statements, judgements, and actions; and 2) empowering new daily rituals for yourself—whatever works for you—to get divinely aligned each day.

Ask the following questions daily:

- Are my thoughts and emotions aligned with my spirits desire for joy, peace, success and abundance?
- Do my words reflect my inner truth?
- Am I being authentic right now?
- Do my actions support the expression of my soul's desire for love, health, harmony and happiness?
- Am I acting according to old beliefs or my soul's truth?
- Are my decisions made from fear or love?

With an honest look at the life you are currently creating, you have the opportunity to allow for new alignment to the divine. This will allow you to align with your dreams and desires, as well as nourish your soul.

The expansive nature of your consciousness determines the quality of your experiences.

Activate your personal power first by aligning to the Divine each and every day.

Drop into Silence

Before awakening, we are in a state of forgetfulness of ourselves, behind the "veil," and seeking to know ourselves. As we seek, we attempt to define ourselves again and again and again and cling to every new definition. Yet we are more than the definitions we find. We are not mere definitions. Our true nature is not defined by human linear words or thoughts. Words are a stepped-down frequency and vibration of a higher energy.

The moment we use words, we start defining things, ourselves, and others. Thoughts precede words. A thought attempts to define energy, especially vibration and frequency. But before the THOUGHT, there is ENERGY, FREQUENCY, and VIBRATION.

We experience energy one of two ways: in its original purity and truth or as a distortion (stepped-down frequency).

Thoughts are triggered by the processor mind to define energy, then words try to define the thoughts, and this thought-word process takes us further and further away from our "pure state" and "higher frequency" abilities. When we resist the temptation to define ourselves and others with thoughts and words, we are free to feel and work with pure energy and to feel what we truly are, which is energy (consciousness).

And the more we do this; the less subtle words and thoughts are. The 'louder' PURE ENERGY becomes to us. Where previously, it was the Mind: the thoughts, the words, the spoken, the written, that was the loudest, and the ENERGY felt very subtle, because the ego Mind was loud (strong).

The key is to drop into silence. The moment we drop into silence, we become sensitive to the pure energy we actually are and the louder the energy becomes—meaning the energy is increasingly physically felt, seen, and heard as a vibration and frequency. The more we choose energy, the more we become our HIGHER SELF. Our higher self is pure energy. It is a concentrated light node of certain individualized geometrical structure. It is not human. It is condensed light (a non-solid energy).

And so, we are guided on our Spiritual Path to drop the noise of thoughts, drop definitions, and talk less, in order to become MORE...the Higher Self which is outside the human experience.

And the more we choose to do this, the stronger the experience and our connection to the Divine becomes.

The higher self is not a personality or another personality to become. This is why one must Un-become and drop aspects of their human personality that are not aligned with the higher self. The higher self does not use human words or have human thoughts; it operates as pure light energy, in a non-gravitational field. It is a concentrated light node energy, capable of merging with infinite energy frequencies and other infinite light nodes to create experiences for its individualized consciousness (for Source/God to experience itself).

PAIN – A channelled text and Activation

"If there is a painful wound, a suffering that is deep, it will bring you back to itself until it is fully met, fully acknowledged and fully resolved."

We are here yes.

While we are here, we are going to read for the collective.

Angelic beings are apparent here and we are going to go up an octave into a higher vibration now.

So, a lot of you may be experiencing new symptoms. This process is a huge shift for you. We have been assisting you with the vibration frequency raising on your planet, as well as your collective and personal space.

We are moving into a time where it is better to just be still. Words are not coming to par over the last few week and months. Words seem to have fallen short in terms of not conveying the true definition of what you are meaning.

That's why feeling is so important right now.

Pause

Pause

Pause

When we stop, we are giving you pauses in energy for you to translate, to feel to interpret, fully without any restraints or vocabulary. But through vibration and attunement.

Many of you are excelling quite quickly now. All of you.

ALL of you. You are so blessed.

When you get on the train to go to a higher track. Any detours are going to frustrate you.

You're going to be like, "Why is this thing or that still here, I let it go!"

And those words alone, those vibrations alone are going to allow that to come back, which will cause these things to stay for a while longer.

So, we are just going to remember here—and we have said it many times— we are just going to reflect on the fact that we must love ourselves right now, as we are. We are also loving everything we perceive as our darkness or our flaws. And then we are going to allow them to go whenever they are ready.

Proceed with the intention to release anything that feels ready to be released. Now.

You have pain, and you wonder, "Why is this pain still here when I have done everything to release and heal it?"

Well first, no you haven't.

There are something's you are overlooking.

And also, you will not be a 100% pain free until we are all pain free. As we are all one.

So why would someone experience chronic pain?

Sometimes we hold onto pain because it is the only feeling we feel safe with. We identify with it; it becomes a part of us. We've used it in our vocabulary so long, that it is like our middle name.

And when we try to remove our middle name, we are going to miss it. You're going to feel naked; you're going to feel raw and exposed.

When you remove pain, you have the feeling that you have this empty space that might be filled with new pain, new hurt. So, you don't allow yourself to let go of the pain, you just keep piling it on, subconsciously.

So how do you let go of subconscious pain?

You first must accept that you will have to go through the uncomfortable separation process. This goes for anger as well. And it is not that comfortable.

Some of you reading this have suppressed anger, rage.

Suppressed anger manifests as rage, where you have moments where you just scream and yell, completely out of line sometimes to block new hurt.

Or you kick something, or throw something. This is not normal behavior, this is learnt, and this is suppressed.

The same as with pain.

Your pain started as an emotion, a feeling, then sunk so deeply into your subconscious that it turned physical.

Suppressed anger is also just on the pathway to physical pain.

So, you disidentify, you unidentify, you remove this attachment to pain.

And you let it go, and you feel raw and you feel bare, and you feel exposed.

And you let go of the pity that attaches you to it.

Let go of Self-loathing. Self-soothing.

Any of those vibrations will carry a vibration that attaches to pain, chronic pain.

Do you know that cancer patients have a similar vibration? All of them.

They have a victim personality trait.

112

That allows these dark energies to attach, of course not like we used to believe. These sticky, dark emotions allow dark energies to attach, clog up our insides, and eventually create disease. If you have any sort of victimhood mentality, you must let it go.

When you don't let go, you invite negative and destructive things to occupy your body. Then you are left to wonder, "Poor me, I wish this never happened, why did this happen?"

We are so fearful to be without our familiar pain, we often say, "Hold me, because I do not know how to feel without this."

Some people suppress and suppress and suppress.

Then comes the physical manifestation. That's when you know it may take a while to release. You must accept it has been there a long time, and it took you, e.g., 35 years to get to that point. But you must let it go.

De-program, unlearn.

So many of you are now in pain.

The letting go process can be much quicker as we continue to learn the teachings of recognizing and releasing. But do not think that just because you were able to let go of your, e.g., painful third birthday party, that you will instantly feel relief. Energy healing will help a lot to surface the buried wounds, but it is your responsibility to go in deeper and deeper and deeper.

Yes, it came from the past, but there is a reason that it is still hanging around in the present. If you weren't still creating it in this present moment, then it would not exist.

So, be aware of your vocabulary. Ask yourself: "What are the words I am saying, putting into the universe, to be brought back into creation?

What thoughts and actions am I putting out there to bring back? What are they?"

With every single word you say, you are creating either more pain or more harmony in your soul. You must catch yourself every single time and ask, "What are these words going to actually accomplish? Do I actually need to call this person out? Do I actually need to say that I was right? Do I actually need to hold them accountable? All to feel better about myself?"

All these things will only hinder your spiritual happiness and prevent you from ascending to freedom and inner peace. What you choose to pursue will feed your present creation. Ask yourself right now: "What negativity am I creating now that I am ready to let go of??

Imagine yourself as a computer program. With your current level of negative thought and word patterns, how many viruses do you create every day to infect yourself?

What words do you continue to say that do not serve you? What tone, what vibration, and what intention do you pursue?

Some of us get so use to our negative patterns that we don't even recognize or realize they're just programmed into us. And that's what we mean by programmed.

You only infect yourself with more viruses when you seek pity for yourself or judge someone else. Generally, it is one extreme to the next, maybe both. You must ask yourself: "What are the intentions of my words to others? Am I just trying to make them feel bad?"

If you're referring to the past or the future, you generally have an ill intention—known or unknown to you.

You might say, "I'm looking forward to tomorrow." Guess what you are saying? You're saying that you don't enjoy right now. You're sending your precious energy to a place you have not yet even occupied.

It is imperative that you are aware of your words. This is why highly evolved beings use telepathic feelings more than vocabulary. When you drop into silence and feel, you won't miss messages intended for you, and you will be very aware of what kind of vibe (negative or positive) you are sending.

For now, since many of you are still using your vocabulary, speaking, you must take care to be impeccable with your words. I know we are coming off as very strict today, but we must be strict because many of you are still seeking to understand why you are still in pain. You are still in pain because of the vibration you are putting out there, because of what you are creating through your intentions, through your words and actions.

It's not karma it's just creation.

It's so, so simple.

But you must be aware. You are awareness, so why would you not be aware?

Be aware of your words and then your actions. Ask yourself, "Why am I doing this or that thing? What energy am I putting and giving out as I vacuum under my husband's legs as he is watching TV.

What is this getting me? Nothing.

We promise you it is nothing. You will only be creating negative energy that divides rather than unites.

We give you signals as to what feels right. Feel it in your body, we give them to you, and so you know what each word is creating. If it feels heavy, it is heavy. Where are you hiding ill intention from yourself?

When you eat ice cream and think it is bad for you and making you fat, why do you think such things? Why is such a thought in your mind? Let it go, it is not the truth. Isn't that wild, it is not the truth.

It is a learnt response. Period.

All right, this is your homework for today: impeccable choice of words.

We want you to use crystal clear words that create positive energy. If you want abundance, every word that comes out of your mouth must be "I am abundance, I choose abundance."

Every single word.

It is done.

"It took profound suffering in order for me to get a little movement in my consciousness. Life did whatever it took to get my attention and Reality is always out to enlighten you in every moment.

Pain ultimately always calls for Presence. One has a choice, either resist or trust."

Riana Arendse

CHAPTER 6:

The Biggest Secret to Enlightenment

The secret no one talks about

Enlightenment is not some fairy tale experience, or something just meant for a few special sacred people. It is the highest peak of our consciousness and is available to all beings in every single moment.

Most of life is defined by the wounded ego - pain and suffering. Those, unfortunately, are the driving forces behind much of what we do (avoiding pain and suffering, and willingly or not inflicting it on others). We feel separate and create the concept of "others or me and them." And we deal with the world by creating illusory mental images that form our unique versions of reality.

But trying to be separate and holding on to other "separate" things (including people) leads to more suffering because nothing is permanent, and life is a continual series of loss and rebirth. Relationships transform and change; people die or move away; objects deteriorate, and so on.

EVERYTHING IS TRANSITORY but because of our fear of being alone and separate, we cling desperately to what we know, to what is familiar, even as we intuitively understand it may not be there tomorrow.

But the greatest secret no one talks about, the one that leads to enlightenment, is this: If you HEAL your relationship with yourself, God, and others, you will ascend to your highest state of consciousness and enlightenment. Period.

Why is this? Because everyone reflects you, they are your mirror. And these relationships will always reflect or mirror parts of you that needs resolution or healing. Parts of you that always arises as triggers or traumas in your day to day life.

By making these relationships your direct mirror of feedback for your healing, you naturally move to higher and higher states of consciousness and frequencies.

The Path to Enlightenment

1. Take an Objective view or way of perceiving the world: See things without expectation, judgment, or preconceived notions. See things as they are. First see things from many different angles or perspectives before you come to a conclusion.

2. Have the right intention: Work from a place of pure intentions (no harm to anyone/ anything). No manipulating.

3. Be Authentic: Say and do what you need to say and do but say and do it from the heart. If you don't know how to get into the heart centre, just think of a moment of bliss. Perhaps the birth of your child or walking on the beach with Jesus, whatever feels of bliss to you. This will immediately shift you into your heart space.

4. Surrender: Complete and fully surrender to the Universe, to Source. Give up your need to control your life or outcome of it and surrender PERMANENTLY. When we surrender to this larger truth, weaving it throughout our day, the most tantalizing and enlightening moments just magically show up. When we completely empty out our cup, the Universe has to fill it. Whenever we are deeply surrendered to life, life surrenders to us. We immediately feel this humble yet empowering connection with everything and everyone. There are no more feelings of lack, unworthiness or separation with who we are. There is also no need to become someone powerful, superior and special, so that we cover up that unconscious insecure self who feels inferior. We can allow all our darker parts to be seen, felt and heard. Life is meant to be a continuous trusting process.

5. Practice Awareness/mindfulness: You become mindful of the most minute, mundane, tiny details of your life experience: the way you talk, the way you stand, the way you walk, your thoughts, your emotions, the way you work, etc. — especially the actions that have become habits. You then also become aware of what others trigger in you, emotions, beliefs and traumas.

6. Be Present: Most of the time, we run on autopilot and our minds are everywhere except the here and now. Presence teaches you to discipline your mind so that it remains HERE and NOW instead of in the past or future.

7. Un-become: Make a commitment to heal all aspects of yourself, personal or inherited, blocks and beliefs. Make the commitment to question all your beliefs and everything you have come to know.

8. Be Open: Know that each experience is always the right experience. For the enlightened being, there is no such thing as a wrong experience. The Universe is the most intelligent teacher there is, and it never ever makes a mistake. This Universe is this grand weave of perpetual spiritual synchronicity and our karmic destiny.

9. Be aware and open to the higher truth that we are all One : If you step back and look at our world from the highest most heavenly space, it appears that we are this great symphony of souls all working together to reach higher states of consciousness. Of course, we are also these separate beings with unique minds, hearts and individual lives. Yet this separating aspect is not the biggest truth. The greatest truth is that we are intimately connected with everything and everyone else in the Universe.

10. Be fearless in unravelling and exposing our most enlightened and horrific selves – our Shadows. We must be able to relax and truly be at ok with every good and bad idea that passes through our mind and emotions. We cannot take anything that is revealed personally, as every idea and concept we have about who we are was handed down to us, programmed in our subconscious mind from our parents, siblings, teachers, society and the many generations who were before them.

11. Rest in silence and stillness of mind. Ironically, the cause of our enlightenment and what's blocking us from experiencing it is the same thing... the mind. When we transcend the mind, dropping any attachment we have to it, the brilliant light of our being can then shine through and this brilliance is all we can see in every direction. Of course, a mind is essential to adventure into this great journey into spiritual liberation, yet we first need to understand what the mind actually is, so that one day we can become free from it. If you start to watch your mind, you'll notice it is always striving, judging, analysing and needing to achieve something. You may have lived your entire life so far, completely wrapped up in the head, which is always focusing on thoughts, concepts, right and wrong opinions, judgments and belief systems. Know that enlightenment is full body experience. This means the whole body is engaged in experiencing life, and not just the over analytical mind. To step back from the mind requires total awareness. Every enlightened experience begins by first taking ONE step back from the mind and resting into a state of pure awareness. Therefore, an enlightenment seeker meditates. Not to control the mind, yet to transcend all thinking completely, calling forth the experience of total silence, stillness and pure awareness inside. Stillness creates an automatic letting go of the constant control, domination and neediness of the mind. It is something that takes 100% of your devotion and dedication, as the mind is deeply addicted to the outer search. It will spend lifetimes searching for fulfilment in the outer world, believing this is the purpose of life. It will continuously try to fill your time on earth with new information, people, and special goodies out there, never questioning reality or what your heart or soul is really yearning for inside. Trust the heart instead of the mind. The heart lives in love and abides in a connection of oneness with the Universe. This is the easiest doorway to enter the experience of enlightenment.

12. Feel the oneness between the spiritual and material world. Manifesting our material dream life and the road to enlightenment are two sides of the same coin. When we embrace our natural manifesting ability, we must also open the doors for a greater spiritual depth inside, which is needed to balance everything out. We cannot be fully enlightened unless we are enjoying our connection with the vibrant rich matrix of powerful manifesting energy that exists in quantum particles all around us and is what we refer to as the material world. We also cannot totally enjoy any physical riches and luxuries of the material world, without being relaxed and surrendered to our divine spiritual energy at our core. These worlds are one world, two sides of the same coin, and they are interdependent with each other, feeding into the other. They cannot exist without each other. If we judge something in the material world as bad, we set up an energetic block inside us which stops our spiritual growth, and vice-versa. It is only through surrendering to the merging of our spiritual and material nature that we find the fastest path to freedom. Ironically, you will find the experience of spiritual surrender is one of the greatest manifesting secrets that was ever invented and causes our dreams and desires to manifest faster than the speed of light.

It's a great cosmic paradox that we are constantly striving to attain our natural, highest state of being when in essence, we are already just that. Therefore, enlightenment is much easier than we think, and our only real effort should be to focus on being 100% effortless.

So, while you will face a few essential tests on the great journey to enlightenment, just remember that your struggles, losses, pains, and facing of your shadows comprise the very fuel that will eventually burn your ego away. Again, the Universe/Source/God has invented the perfect spiritual path to enlightenment.

Always know the Divine Universe never makes mistakes. The spirit pulling you deeper into this very moment of your life is revealing the real reason you are here. If you look for your enlightenment path anywhere other than the now, you'll miss it. It is hidden in the most sacred place that you are least likely to look for it.

CHAPTER 7:

Remembering

Focusing on truths already known to you

The truths you are seeking are already known within you. The awakening journey is not about finding something new, but about remembering and coming to know existent truths.

When each of us decides to incarnate into this reality, the moment we take our first breath, we forget truths we already know... on purpose. We forget the "source" of all that is us. The reason we do this is so we can experience a specific lesson or desire in this life. The lessons and experiences we wish to have in this life inevitably help us find our way back to who we truly are.

The truths I will reveal within the following steps and texts, I believe is most important to remember or awaken to when one embarks on a healing, un-becoming journey of mastery, because without these truths, you cannot fully remember and actualize the POWER within yourself.

These truths will change the game for all of us, once we awaken to it. As there will be no more opportunity for blame, confusion or victimization. But only the choice to remember the power inherent within ourselves.

First, you must take responsibility for your creations thus far and let go of your stories. Letting go of victimhood and powerlessness is required to empower yourself, shift your reality, and change your story.

We cannot fully heal and step into our true nature, without taking full responsibility for everything we have ever experienced in our lives. Period.

The purpose of this book is not only to bring truth forth but also to share tools you can utilize to apply spiritual wisdom to your day-to-day life.

What causes the most suffering is not being able to truly be who you are. And one way to truly step into the truth of you is to Un-become and strip away all that is untruth. If fear is holding you back from taking this step, fear of judgement from others, fear of not fitting in, I say to you this; only when you require no approval from outside yourself, can you really own your true self, are you then able to truly go back to Love.

You are being called now to a new life, to a truth and remembering, a whole new level of awareness of who and what you are. Allow yourself to make the commitment to Un-become, to expand yourself to a new level of consciousness.

Should you choose to continue reading this book of Un-becoming, the process of remembering will begin working in your soul. As you remember truths, you will feel as though a light has been switched on permanently inside you. You will feel a sort of unconscious restlessness, and it will push you further along the journey until your external reality begins reflecting new truths and creations.

To help you progress on your Un-becoming and healing journey, in the next steps and texts I will reveal truths to remember so you can be attuned to a higher vibration. There are many more truths, however these particular truths will positively change the trajectory of your way of being, believing, and seeing. Once these truths are known, remembered, and awakened, no matter how stubborn your old beliefs, you will have subconscious knowledge and begin to question everything you have ever come to believe in this life.

THE TIME SPACE REALITY WE KNOW IS AN ILLUSION

Time and space, as we have come to know it, are illusions. From a universal perspective, time does not exist.

The theory, which is backed up Albert Einstein's theory of relativity, states that space and time are part of a four-dimensional structure where everything that has happened has its own co-ordinates in space-time.

What does that mean in simple English? It means your past, present and future are happening simultaneously, at this very moment. It means that the six-year-old you still exists. And if the six-year-old you still exists, that six-year-old is helping to create your current reality. So how is it that one can go back to the past in one's mind or imagination, to heal the inner child and that healing can take place in our present selves today?

Because the past, present and future is happening simultaneously at this very moment. This would mean that time is not linear, as we have come to believe, but rather everything is ever present.

So, instead of thinking that time and events sail past you and then completely vanish, it is better to think that they still exist, and are existing simultaneously, in distinct parts of space-time. It's just that you can't access anything outside of the present block you are in. Your younger self is living as you are living presently, but in a different dimension.

When you heal or change something from the past you are literally shifting the timelines and healing yourself in the now. Your younger selves is living as you are living presently, but in a totally different dimension.

126

When we look at time in a linear way, it is easy to think that we have no capacity to change the past or that all that really exists is now, or that the future is decided, like fate. This universe is governed according to the law of attraction; this includes time.

It is the state whereby things that are of like frequency are drawn together like a magnet. Like a mirror, what we experience in the world is a reflection of what is inside of us, both conscious and subconscious. For example, a person who has low self-esteem, attracts circumstances, people, places, and events etc. that are a match to the vibration of low self-esteem. Cause and effect are simply the way that the law of attraction manifests on a physical level.

Any time we alter a cause, we alter the effect. This means, any time we make a change to what is within us, what is outside of us changes too. When we alter our vibration, it changes what is reflected in this universe of mirroring.

When this is the case, it is easy to see that the future is never set in stone. If a person changes something that is in the current moment, they change what they are a vibrational match to in the future. At this level, fate does not exist. The future exists in a state of potentiality and possibility. Because of this, it is accurate to say that the future both exists and at the same time, does not exist.

It is helpful to gain insights about what you are lining up with in the future, based on where you are today, but never use such insights to fall into the illusion that you are powerless to alter the future. Anything you do today sets in motion a vibrational momentum that pre-paves and determines your future. And so, the future really is in your hands.

You are the creator of it all.

DESTINY VS DESIRE

You might be wondering: "Can I really choose what I want, or is my destiny already decided?"

What if I told you that you already have everything you desire and dream of?

The future desires you have now—which are in alignment with the desires your higher self has for you—are already yours. They are desires based on a future reality that awaits you. Isn't that absolutely amazing to know??

In essence, you already have what you desire, as your future self, and the only thing you now must do is line up with it—by vibrationally becoming a match to it.

Allow me to reiterate this - *Your desires and dreams are already yours.*

They don't seem so far out of reach now, do they?

This means that your desires has to be yours, it must be yours. Period.

If, at the time you are hearing this message, you are not currently living a life that makes you feel a deep, fulfilling sense of purpose, it is understandable. This is common battle we all fight in a modern society that conditions us to adopt external values, opinions, and advice from people around us to succeed. We do this for one primary reason: to cling to the illusion that happiness, worth, security, love, care, and direction come from others—when in fact those things can only come from our true selves.

In general, people do not understand how the future really works. Since time doesn't actually exist, destiny is nothing more than potential your higher self has selected (either consciously or subconsciously) to vibrationally align with. But free will is an absolute of our existence. This means that your future is an ocean of potentials, some more probable than others. The important truth to know is that any single change you make will alter those potentials and therefore alter your future life.

As you breathe now, you will receive a pouring forth of this elixir to allow the Christ consciousness within you to open more deeply.

As you do this, fill yourself through every chakra, organ, meridian, cell, and light bodies, now.

HOW TO UN-BECOME, THE PROCESS (SELF MASTERY & HEALING)

You will not incarnate into a higher vibration without work on your part. Nothing will solve all your problems and move you into a higher dimensional reality without you taking responsibility for your creations.

What you have created is your responsibility and you are being guided now by the divine, the universe, God, who will support you as you grow and change and reclaim your manifestation as the Creator fully embodied as you.

If you believe there is a God, and that He is saying no to you and rejecting your desires and wants all the time, then that will be your experience. Whatever you believe will be your manifestation. When you know the power that lies within you, you will truly begin to Un-become, truly begin to heal, and truly return to the source of all that is—within.

To fully embody your God essence in this reality, you must align yourself to the truth of who you truly are. To do that, you must discard everything that is not part of the higher truth of you, in your body and subconscious mind. This process leads to healing. You might be wondering:

"How do I know what to heal?" I will answer this question for you in a bit.

For now, just know that once healing is complete, you will still need to consciously choose different thoughts and choices each day. You must get out of the habit of living from a reactive space based on past experiences and fully live in the now moment. Be present most of the time. All of this requires self-mastery, and that is what I am ultimately teaching and guiding you in this book. These are the very techniques I use on a daily basis in order to embody my true essence and integrate truth into my being and life more every day.

It's important to recognize there are aspects of you that live simultaneously in this reality and in higher dimensions. The aspect of you that lives at the higher spiritual level is called your "higher self." In the next section, I have shared a step-by-step process to help you access your higher self. By making changes at the higher level first, you will be sowing seeds for positive change to occur in the reality you live in now.

Physical change, healing, and transformation must first occur in the spiritual spaces of Higher Power, Higher Embodiment, and Higher Knowing. We cannot heal ourselves by and through the "small self, because the small self still sees lack, unhappiness, and illusion where the higher self does not. The higher self sees only the truth of what is. The higher self, which I also call the "God Self," is who we truly are.

As you begin to develop and integrate the tools I've shared into your daily life, your consciousness will evolve and transform, your challenges will begin to dissipate, and you will become consciously aware of more than you ever could have imagined. The veil of illusion will begin to lift, and you will begin to see Oneness in all things.

This powerful, step-by-step process I have formulated is the exact process I have used to transform my life from deep suffering to absolute love—love that persists no matter what is going on outside of myself. It is through this transformative process that I have come to see everything, everyone, and every situation as a GIFT. As you follow this process, I'm confident that you also will start to see that everything is an opportunity and not a burden. Only the small self thinks of things and people as burdens.

You will learn that your real Power comes from within you, and you will learn to rely on your own intuition, your own inner knowingness. It is a wonderful thing to be able to be in the universal flow of life of the divine. Because what we truly want is to find ourselves, to know ourselves and to remember who we are.

And we say to you today…. you will.

For most of us, we look for fulfilment outside of ourselves. We look for it within relationships with others, with a partner, in our jobs and careers, we look for it in what we have achieved and what we have accumulated over the years. But still there still seems to be that void.

And for one who has already awakened, the struggle does not end there. The awakening is just a wakeup call, this book is your wake-up call. And from there the actual conscious work begins.

With the help of my guides, the collective of our higher selves, ascended masters, and the Source of all, I have developed this step by step approach to Mastering oneself, a modality also to Heal oneself instantly, which has proven itself useful to my myself, my clients and my students.

When understood, practiced and mastered, these concepts will help you create the life you yearn for. It will become the tools you use to recreate yourself over and over each time to a higher degree of consciousness.

It is an Un-becoming of all that you were, all that you thought you had to be, it is a complete surrender of the small self.

SELF MASTERY & HEALING

"Be still...collect wisdom through awareness."

STEP 1 – THE ART OF AWARENESS

Observing the Self

Ask yourself this question: "Who am I?"

Perfect.

Now ask yourself this: "Who is watching, aware of, and observing all my thoughts?" You are the one who is noticing all these thoughts, the voices in your mind and these inner disturbances.

Just watch.

Just observe.

The mere fact that you are aware of these thoughts, these inner conflicts, means that you are not it, you are the observer of it.

Observation/Awareness will transform your life.

It is a tool I use every single day since I have begun my journey of Un-becoming. The art of Awareness is a process by which you begin to witness yourself and others very intently. It is the process by which we begin to explore our own being in order to become whole and integrate all aspects of us into wholeness again.

As Source, as a Spiritual being; you know all things, each of you holds the answers and yet the disintegration of yourself builds barriers to becoming whole and to BEING. It is these fractured and disassociated parts that separates us from spirit. And so, Awareness is the first and most crucial step in healing and mastering ourselves.

Awareness enables you to return to the state of beingness, where you can just be. From there, you will discover and remember who you are and let go of your attachments.

Put aside all restrictions and limitations and allow yourself to simply be.

Begin to examine your own thoughts, feelings, and experiences to reach understanding of spiritual awareness. The more aware you are, the greater your understanding, compassion, and respect for the world and all things in it. Only then can you can rise above feelings of greed, hatred, jealousy, resentfulness, and despair. You will be calmer, more at peace, and have an understanding about your higher life purpose.

Spiritual awareness will also positively impact your health, decreasing the likelihood of suffering from stress, anxiety and depression. Meditation is often useful for those seeking to become more spiritually aware, as it clears the mind and removes clutter, allowing for true and calm inner reflection and understanding. It also helps people to release fears and change negative thought patterns, both of which are essential to becoming aware.

This is not to say that you should live the life of loneliness, but rather that you should feel content within yourself, fulfilled by yourself and able to create your own happiness instead of relying on other people or things to make you feel complete or worthy. This will however come at a later stage when we have reached a state of higher Awareness.

Live the life that you want to live. Live it with regard to other people, but not for other people. Stop worrying about what society expects from you, and do not bend to accommodate the demands of society if they are not true to your beliefs.

As we've already discussed, a sense of peace and belonging is one of the most important benefits of learning how to tap into higher levels of spiritual awareness. The desire for material possessions takes a back seat to higher spiritual things that money just can't buy.

When you're able to expand your spiritual awareness, you begin to realize that you are in total control of creating the life you live. And rather than seeing that as something to fear, you find it is, in fact, freeing.

Humility, compassion, understanding — these are all manifestations of spiritual awareness. Whether they develop over time or occur almost overnight depends on the catalyst that precedes this awakening and your receptiveness at that specific moment.

In addition to the awareness tools I will be sharing, the following practices will increase your awareness and spirituality in general.

- Meditation/Stillness
- Being honest with yourself about yourself and what others trigger within you
- Practice forgiveness and compassion for self and others
- Spend time in nature
- Concentrate on expanding your mind – binaural beats or guided meditations
- This is a big one: Question ALL your beliefs and all your perceptual truths that you have based on past experiences

and what you have been taught by your parents and by society. EVERY SINGLE ONE. This includes your religion, your beliefs about God, about this world, about Love, Money and so on.

As awareness begins to grow and cultivate, some people begin to think that things are getting worse, but what is happening is they are actually becoming more aware of what has been lurking underneath, more aware and conscious of what has been there all along.

To be sure, you most likely have been living unconsciously, in the sleep state. One may still find that they are still being triggered by others, colleagues, partner, parents and children, and seeing reactive patterns within themselves still being perpetuated.

The reactive triggers and patterns will not simply disappear overnight, you'll just be more aware of them. Don't worry; though your reactive triggers and patterns will not disappear overnight, you will become more aware of them and have the ability to objectively see them rather than embody them.

So, while you will continue to be triggered for a while (and experience the negative reactive emotions due to the trigger), the awareness you are practicing will eventually expand your levels of consciousness. Don't resist the process. Triggers inform you the wound is still there. This is good. Why? Because it allow you to begin expanding on what is being mirrored to you.

Fortunately, the time gap between the actual event and the return of awareness tends to get shorter as you become more present. The great step forward is when, in the middle of being triggered, you become consciously aware you are being triggered. Consciousness.

So, whenever you discover a dysfunctional, unconscious pattern in yourself, it doesn't mean you've failed; it means you're there. It's always a great thing to see it in yourself. It is the Gift that allows you to now go within, heal what it is and bring it back into wholeness again.

At its best, is when you are aware of the voice inside your head, and you can see your old patterns, as if you are looking at yourself from a bird's eye perspective. You are no longer the emotion but observing it.

Awareness must be practiced every day, in every situation, starting the moment you wake up in the morning. Period.

STEP 1.1 - AWARENESS – INTERNAL THOUGHTS AND INTENTIONS

"Your relationship with these mind-made stories are what causes you suffering.

And I say to you.

Let it go..."

Before we can begin to look at our external reality, we need to first master the art of internal awareness. Our mind chatter, our thoughts, and begin to remain within the self.

Your thoughts shape your identity — those fragments of mind which pass through your brain a million times a day, create the fundamental person that is you. If you are not convinced of this, recall your last angry thought and note how it affected your physiology. One's inclination toward stress nowadays stems from recurring restless thoughts which become stuck in a feedback loop.

To change our default setting, we must measure the impact of our thoughts. Consider your answers to the following questions:

When do disempowering thoughts surface? Is it when you're tired, hungry, or emotional?

136

What is the theme of those thoughts? Are they self-deprecating, shameful, or resentful?

In this step, we will dive into a few exercises that will allow you to meditatively experience self-awareness and presence.

For a moment now, find a place to just sit in stillness, and close your eyes. Become really aware of your thoughts, almost like a higher perspective of you watching your thoughts go by.

Do this now.

......

What thoughts did you observe?

If you were unable to become aware of your thoughts, be in stillness again for 5 minutes and then when done, reflect on what thoughts you remember arising for you.

10-day exercise:

1. Create a Thoughts journal for the next 10 days. Writing down what your prominent thoughts are for the day, grouping your thoughts together to see what you are sending out into the universe, paying attention to any negative thoughts or thought loops.
2. Getting to know yourself through thought reflection. Whatever you send out through thought, word and action you attract back to you. Change your thoughts change your reality!
3. Stop and listen to your body. Tune into which areas are hurting or tight or uncomfortable. Ask for a signal to the areas that need attention, then stop and listen for a response. It may be easier to write it down. Listen and then write the first word that comes to you.

4. Paying attention to any intrusive thoughts, stopping them in their tracks but seeing what they are trying to tell you. Being aware of how much you get distracted, daydream or have thought loops or negative thoughts.
5. Now say the following whenever these thoughts arise, I now release and transmute any and all limited beliefs, low vibrational thoughts, past traumas and triggers, supressed emotions and all that does not have my highest good in mind in love and light to be blessed, cleared and transmuted to the highest vibration of love and light.
6. When you are unsure of what to do or trying to live your highest life, simply ask:
   a. "What would love do or what would God do?"
7. Detach from your thoughts, become the observer
8. Practice Mindfulness
9. Practice Self Compassion
10. Clear negative thoughts and replace them with new beliefs.

Whether we see ourselves as victims, heroes, or bad people, we all define ourselves though the lens of our stories. We all live through the lines of the narratives we tell ourselves, and yet the truth is so much greater than any of our stories.

Presence Exercise:

1. Look for 3 blue things within the room that you are in.
2. Touch 2 black things in your room
3. Listen to 2 different sounds now

What did you feel? Did you feel yourself being present there?

THE POWER OF INTENTION

The POWER of intention! Things are manifesting SO quickly now! Don't leave yourself room for regret later by succumbing to old patterns and using old vocabulary. Our words are SO important. What are our words intending? Better yet, what are WE intending? What is the word describing the feeling we are sending out? You may have done this so much that you do it out of habit rather than awareness.

Ask yourself:

Is my intention in doing this to get what I want?

Is my intention in saying this to make them feel bad?

Is my intention in doing or saying this to create conflict?

Is my intention in doing this or saying this to prove that I'm right?

Is my intention in doing this to make myself feel better?

Is my intention in doing this to sabotage my happiness?

Is my intention in doing this to create suffering?

Is my intention in doing this or saying this, to make me look better?

What is my intention?

STEP 1.2 - EMOTIONAL AWARENESS/EMOTIONAL HEALTH

What does this mean?

This step will help you listen and become aware of the emotions that are sparked by interactions with others.

Every single emotion is necessary and important, even the challenging ones. Emotions are an indicator that something is not okay. You must get in the habit of learning to understand and love your emotions and discover how they serve you. Your emotions are a guidance system, a gift in and of itself, which allow you to make clear decisions and begin to heal.

Emotional health underpins our physical and our mental health. If you are really stressed and emotionally charged, it will really create negative patterns of thinking. You are more likely to come down with a cold too, as it lowers your immune system.

Emotions are one of the most important aspects of healing and self-mastery. Understanding how they serve you, and what they are communicating to you, is the first step. Learning to use your emotions as a guidance system, through awareness, can be life changing.

When your emotions run high, retreat (if possible), be calm, and contemplate—not to run and hide, but to allow yourself to step away, meditate, and evaluate your emotions. Doing this will allow you to step out of your small self into your higher self. This is the process by which you will move into higher levels of consciousness.

Ask the following questions when we feel an intense emotion:

How do I feel right now?

Why do I feel this way?

Where do I think these feeling stems from if I think back to my childhood?

What is the belief that I might have behind this emotion?

STEP 2 – AWARENESS – EVERYONE IS YOUR MIRROR

"The world you perceive and experience, is but a reflection of the world within you. You are continually shaping the world around you as a result of conscious and unconscious thoughts. Being the master of your fate - should you resign yourself to victim or perpetrator, to your stories, your beliefs and judgements, life will certainly offer you evidence of this. Reality merely provides confirmation of your thoughts and all you can see when you look out into the world is your own thinking and beliefs reflected back to you in the mirror of your level of your self-consciousness. If you entertain distorted thoughts and beliefs, correct them to align with the truth."

Riana Arendse

This step (Awareness) will be the hardest to fathom if you have been conditioned to believe consciously or subconsciously that you are a victim, and that everything happening to you is the fault of others.

When the Divine bestowed this universal truth on me—the law of mirroring or the law of resonance and attraction—I instantly remembered who I was. It was then I could see how my reality was the projection of my unconscious, unhealed and out of alignment to the truth of who I truly was/am.

So, when you accept this truth and use it as part of your daily healing and self-mastery tools, you will instantly begin to see what is out of alignment with you and begin to realize there really is no victim and perpetrator. You will see that what you see and what is constantly triggered within you is mirrored in all people and all situations that you are attracting into your life and your reality.

Everyone is Your Mirror.

The Greatest Relationship Secret. Everyone is your mirror.

This is the greatest relationship secret. Everyone is your mirror. This is the greatest of all life secrets and the only one you really need to understand to transform your life and all your relationships.

Every single person in your life is your mirror. What this means is that others are simply reflecting parts of your own consciousness back to you, giving you an opportunity to really see yourself and ultimately to heal and grow. The qualities you most admire in others are your own and the same goes for those qualities you dislike.

To change anything in your relationships, one must heal all those aspects of ourselves, one must look inward first. Learning to recognise yourself in others is the biggest step in awareness that needs to be practiced daily, moment to moment consistently – especially when you are being triggered.

Everything and everyone is your mirror. Only when you begin truly seeing yourself reflected back at you will you be FREE—free from seeking blame, free from making judgments, and free from being the victim of another person's actions or words. This truth applies to everyone you encounter: your friends, family, and colleagues, and even to those that you cannot stand. It is through your relationship with others that you will come to see the closest, most accurate image of who you are.

What are You Really Seeing in the Mirror?

To internalise this truth, that everyone is your mirror, you must first understand it. Your relationships with others are your opportunity to see yourself, experience yourself and to really become aware of what is being triggered within you.

They are a perfect mirror of your inner relationship with yourself and the beliefs you have acquired throughout your life. Everything you admire in another person belongs to you and the same goes for all that which you dislike. In order for you to recognise a certain quality in another, then it must be part of your consciousness, a part of you. You could not see it otherwise. No matter how pleasant or painful a relationship is, other people are your mirrors. Everyone in your life reflects some aspects of you. Be it an irritated postman, loving spouse, or an envious friend. Others reflect especially those parts of you that you aren't willing to see.

Your Beliefs are Staring You in the Face.

Your beliefs about relationships, about men, about women, about love and life in general, are there for you to see in the mirror of your all your relationships, but mostly in your most intimate relationship. This is why intimate relationships can be so painful and hurtful.

We have all acquired certain beliefs throughout our lifetime that cause us to react and act in certain habitual ways that do or don't support us. Your beliefs were instilled at a young age. You may have a subconscious belief that you are unworthy of love or that your childhood definition love is limited and conditional. With limited beliefs about love, you will attract a partner who will trigger feelings of worthlessness or being unloved, or one whose love has conditions. Whatever the case, this toxic cycle—a different face and different situation, but the same pattern—will continue until you break it.

It's important to understand you did not consciously choose many of the beliefs that govern your experiences and relationships at the subconscious level. Instead, your beliefs were, unbeknownst to you, instilled in you by your parents, society, the media, friends, culture, and upbringing. Since your relationships mirror and trigger those beliefs, your experiences only prove to re-enforce them, thereby creating an ongoing cycle.

Emotionally and physically abusive relationships are no exception. As you have read in my early life story, I had attracted numerous sexual assaults, sexual abuse, and torment from both people I was in relationships with and strangers. Their reflection is no less accurate than that of any other relationship.

At the root of abusive relationships, you will usually find a severe lack of self-worth in the abused partner, which is evidenced in their refusal to leave the abuser. The only way to rise above such relationships is through the power of self-love.

In fact, it is the foundation of this great secret that everyone is your mirror.

When we want to change someone, we're trying to change ourselves— the reflection of ourselves that we don't like. Attempting to change someone is like looking into the mirror and trying to explain to the mirror that we don't like what we see. It simply doesn't work, and we miss the valuable gift and lesson inherent in that mirror: the relationship. Instead of wasting our time, we can accept what others mirror back to us.

In essence, we must Un-become the illusion, the beliefs, and the blocks that prevent us from attracting the type of relationships we desire. In order to know what unconditional love feels like, we must first experience it and believe it within ourselves.

You're the common factor in all of your relationships. You are the Revelation!

Therefore, going from one relationship into another without understanding why you unconsciously attracted it or attract similar partners doesn't help. It leads to the same results.

Learn to read what others reflect you, below are a few examples:

- People get upset with you
- If people get often upset with you, examine whether you're unconsciously mad at the world or yourself. If you encounter angry and irritated people, they mirror your anger. You might not recognize that you're angry, but others pick up our energy regardless. One of the relationships that I attracted into my reality was a man who was extremely angry at me, I didn't understand how he could be mirroring me, as I am not an angry person at all. I am calm, easy going and empathic. But when I really began questioning what this could be, I came to the realization that he was mirroring an aspect of me that was not allowed to be angry. As a child I believed I needed to supress my emotions, that it was wrong to express negative emotions. And so instead I supressed it, and never expressed how I truly felt. I held everything within until this point. And what I needed to do was bring that fractured little girl into me, welcoming her and allowing her to freely express herself. When I did that, I immediately felt as though my throat chakra had opened so wide. I had never heard my voice this strong and this loud before.
- Others don't believe in your dreams
- If this is your case, then ask yourself whether YOU believe in your dreams. Are you 100% committed to them?
- How do you speak about what you want – is there a sense of lack of trust?

- Others only reflect your inner doubts, your inauthenticity. Especially when you choose a path that you feel obligated to go into, doing something not out of love or passion but because you had to. It has happened to most of us that the closest people who were "supposed" to support us were questioning if what we do is the right thing.
- Don't take it as a sign that what you do is wrong. Instead, shift your perception to see that you need to support your dreams more.
- People tell you what you should do
- Sometimes it's normal that others tell you what you need to do — like in work. But if your partner, family, or friends tell you way too often what you should do, then it reflects a fear of making your own decisions. Lack of self-trust and inner knowing. Others can feel whether we trust our opinions.
- Your partner constantly makes you feel like you are less, not important, and underappreciated. Constant criticism. This is a common one most people struggle with in their intimate relationships. This is a direct mirror of lack of self-love, self-compassion, self-criticism, self-judgement, and self-worth
- Others are doing what you want to do. When you notice people doing all the things you wish you were doing (for example, taking dance classes, language courses, or holding a job that you've wanted) it's a clear wake-up call. It means that you can do it yourself, but for some reason, you don't. Others are showing you that it can be done. It should be your motivation to take the first step. They are mirroring your potential in this life. Whatever you admire in others is also within you.

Begin to practice becoming aware of what others are mirroring about yourself.

If it seems too difficult, ask yourself the following questions:

- What emotion did that trigger in me?
- How did it make me feel? This is your opportunity to bring the feelings to your conscious awareness
- How do I feel right now?
- How do I feel within myself right now?
- What is that deep feeling about myself that attracted this situation into my reality?
- What is the lesson my soul wants me to learn right now?

You can take anyone and see what they reflect you about yourself. Some reflections show what we need to heal while others are meant to inspire us to step up. People you meet are either your teacher or mirror. However, I see those that are my mirrors are my teachers too.

Once you shift your perception about your relationships, you can have more fun. Instead of blaming someone, you can think; oh, that's interesting information. Thank you, I'll support myself more. This awareness process allows us to place our attention on how we are feeling so that we can recognize what deep unresolved past wound is unhealed within us and is thus continuing to mirror itself in our lives.

STEP 3 – AWARENESS OF TRIGGERS

So, what are emotional triggers? When we have strong, emotional reactions to things, it means that a past trauma has been triggered. Eckhart Tolle refers to the part of you that is being triggered as the "pain body" or "emotional body."

The pain body is an accumulation of old emotional pains and life experiences living inside you that were not fully faced and accepted when they arose. Unaddressed traumatic experiences leave behind energy in the form of emotional pain. One by one, each new energy form sticks with other energy forms, and eventually they form a "pain body." When we have a strong emotional reaction to something, the strong reaction means that our past trauma has been triggered.

The pain body becomes active when something triggers a very strong emotional reaction. At that moment, the emotion takes over your mind, your internal dialogue (which is dysfunctional even in the best of times), and the pain body's voice becomes your inner voice. Everything it says is deeply colored by the old, painful emotion of the pain body. Every interpretation, every judgment about your life, about other people, about a situation you are in, will be totally distorted by the old emotional pain.

We all have emotional triggers. You know the feeling you get when someone makes a mean comment that might not be a huge deal to another person but totally destabilizes you for the rest of the day? Perhaps you feel this way when someone expresses disapproval of you? Suddenly, you find yourself feeling off-centre and thrust into anxiety, fear, or even anger? These are the bad fruits of emotional triggers.

Emotional triggers are people, words, opinions, situations, or environmental situations that provoke an intense and excessive emotional reaction within us. Common emotions we experience while being triggered include: anger, rage, sadness, and fear. Virtually anything can trigger us. Depending on our beliefs, values, and earlier life experiences (such as a tone of voice, a type of person, a viewpoint, a single word), anything can be a trigger. Sound familiar?

It can be challenging to identify what exactly our triggers are, but this process of getting to know and understand them can help us heal and learn how to cope better in response.

But why do we all have triggers? In short, because we were all children once. When we were growing up, we inevitably experienced pain or suffering that we could not acknowledge and/or deal with sufficiently at the time. So as adults, we typically become triggered by experiences that are reminiscent of these old painful feelings. As a result, we typically turn to a habitual or addictive way of trying to manage the painful feelings.

Once you know your triggers, you can consider the origins of them and begin to shift them.

So, what are your triggers?

What do you do to manage the painful feelings that are triggered?

Do you face your triggers head-on or attempt to avoid the pain?

Here are a few examples that might help you to discover your own triggers.

Do any of these situations trigger you? Identifying your triggers is the first step to healing from them.

- Someone rejecting you.
- Someone leaving you (or the threat that they will).
- Helplessness over painful situations.
- Someone discounting or ignoring you.
- Someone being unavailable to you.
- Someone giving you a disapproving look.
- Someone blaming or shaming you.
- Someone being judgmental or critical of you.
- Someone being too busy to make time for you.
- Someone not appearing to be happy to see you.
- Someone coming on to you sexually in a needy way.
- Someone trying to control you.
- Someone being needy or trying to smother you.

Once you know your triggers, you can consider the origins of them. If you identify with any of these, ask yourself what they might relate to from your childhood experiences.

We suffer from emotional triggers for three main reasons:

- **Conflicting Conscious and Subconscious beliefs and values–** When we are strongly identified with a certain belief, we may find it hard to be tolerant of other opposing beliefs. For example, there's a reason why religion is such a triggering topic for so many people: beliefs give us a sense of safety and comfort, and when they are challenged, we feel (from an emotional and psychological standpoint) like our lives are being put in danger. Values stem from beliefs and involve what we hold as important in life. When another person disagrees or challenges our values, we get triggered because they are calling into question the truth and legitimacy of what we hold dear.

- **Trauma (the emotional body)** – Getting "triggered" is a term that traces back to the experiences of post-traumatic stress disorder (PTSD) often experienced by anyone who has experienced intense trauma. When we are triggered due to past traumatic experiences, our reaction is often extreme fear and panic (or in some cases, anger). We get triggered when we see, hear, taste, touch, or smell something that reminds us of the previous traumatic circumstance. For example, a rape victim might be triggered when she sees men with beards because her abuser also had a beard. A man who was assaulted by his alcoholic mother as a child might be triggered whenever he smells alcohol. An adult who never fit in as a child may feel triggered when seeing groups of people have fun.

- **Preserving the Ego** – The ego is the sense of self or 'I' we carry around. This manmade identity that we carry is composed of thoughts, memories, cultural values, assumptions, and belief structures that we have developed in order to fit into society. We all have an ego and its primary purpose is to protect us by developing elaborate 'self-protection' mechanisms in the form of beliefs, ideals, desires, habits, and addictions (in order to prevent us from facing what we fear the most: the death of ego or self). When our egos are challenged or hurt by others, we are prone to becoming triggered – immediately. We will argue, insult, belittle, defame, backstab, sabotage, assault, and even murder (in extreme circumstances) people who pose a threat to our ego's survival. The only way to be liberated from our egos, to experience permanent ego integration, is to do some deep inner shadow work, and master awareness. Most importantly, we must connect to the Source of who we are and understand that we are all one and there is no separation. Only then can we operate predominantly from the heart instead of the mind.

So, what do we do when we are triggered?

Firstly, we become aware of what this emotion or belief is that has been triggered. We become aware of what in our Emotional/Pain body has been triggered? What is the underlying emotion? Recall these questions from the previous chapter on mirrors.

- What emotion did that trigger in me? And why?
- How did it make me feel? And why? This is your opportunity to bring the feelings to your conscious awareness
- How do I feel right now and why?

151

- How do I feel within myself right now?
- What is that deep feeling about myself that attracted this situation into my reality?
- What is the lesson my soul wants me to learn right now?

So, let's just recap on what we have covered here:

- Everyone is our mirror, all aspects good and bad, light and dark, positive and negative. We have an emotional body/pain body where all of our past traumas, experiences and hurts are stored. This Emotional body gets triggered by people who are our mirrors. And so, you see it is interlinked, our Pain Body or Emotional body is a part of ourselves that is still fractured/unhealed/tormented. And remember our mirrors, will reflect all our unconscious, unhealed aspects to us. And these reflections will trigger our Pain Body. So, in essence, when we heal our Pain body/Emotional Body, we can no longer be triggered. We are then brought back into wholeness and into alignment with who we are. We can choose beliefs that are more positive about ourselves. And in turn our energetic vibration raises to a higher and higher state of consciousness. We will then no longer be magnets for the hurts we previously experienced. The mirror we see in others will no longer reflect the same things it did before. We will no longer perpetuate the same negative situations and same cycles over and over again. ▢

STEP 4 – AWARENESS OF CONSCIOUS PERCEPTUAL FILTERS

Conscious perceptual filtering can be a bit tricky to understand, so I will give you a personal example to explain what it is and what it reflects about each of us.

I remember during one of my previous romantic relationships, we never would see eye to eye on anything really. The common theme that would occur was that we never saw things the same way. He would experience a different situation than I did, but yet we witnessed the same event. I also noticed in other instances how a friend of mine viewed a comment made by another as nasty and insensitive, but from my perspective, the person was not being insensitive, in fact they were being sensitive. The way in which I perceived that person's actions or behaviors was completely different to the way my friend perceived it. It dawned on me that we were both seeing things through the filtered lens of our own pain bodies and triggers—through our perceptual filtered lenses.

How is this possible?

Most suffering is due to our thoughts about circumstances rather than the circumstances themselves. In fact, the world is merely a projection of our thoughts. Everything we go through is filtered through our pain body and subconscious beliefs. We see things either through the mind of love or the mind of fear. We also have a lens through which we see and experience the world; a lens that acts a filter, disseminating and often adjusting our perception of reality, combining bits of information we process and subsequently respond to.

That lens obtains information that supports whatever perspective we maintain in any given moment. If we are happy, we may identify and relate to happy experiences. If we are sad, we may fixate upon sad events to commiserate with. Much like getting our eyeglasses or contact lenses adjusted, our field of vision (as determined by the lens through which we see the world) can be blurry, convoluted, muddled, or simply distorted. The window through which we process information and transition beyond our current or historical perspective becomes foggy at best.

Imagine you awake in the morning with a negative point of view desperately seeking happiness, yet as a result of the filter through which you experience life, you are unable to access the positive vibrations around you which would actually assist you in shifting your perspective, and instead see continual reminders of the negativity surrounding you.

How can you tell if your filter is distorting your perception of reality?

Before you obsess with your next steps in life, take a moment to analyze the filter through which you see the world. This list is by no means conclusive but ask yourself the following questions as a starting point to help you determine where you lie in the spectrum.

- Irrespective of your actual reality, do you naturally fixate on drama or negativity?
- Is your perception one that supports your victimhood, your pettiness, or your mediocrity? Or one that supports your greatness.
- Regardless of what is spoken from others, are you inclined to misinterpret, overreact, or misunderstand and get frustrated in the process?
- Are you gathering support for the lack in your life, or naturally focusing on the abundance around you?
- Do you regularly complain about situations that don't live up to your expectations?
- Are you constantly reminding yourself of how you think life should be different?

We each experience life from our own perspective... We see what we choose to see—until we shift our perception point. Consider all angles before accepting what you see, as Truth. This process of becoming aware of our Perceptual Filters through which we see others and the world, will allow us to begin shifting from primary identification with the suffering small self to identification with the spiritual higher self.

Most importantly remember this: The views and judgments that other people have of you, their perception of you, has nothing to do with you, but has everything to do with them. So do not take things personally. Come back to this important awareness of Perceptual Filters, remain in the heart space and become aware that everyone sees things through their own filtered lenses.

STEP 5 - CLARITY

This step allows us now to review what we have observed and become aware of ourselves through our interactions with others. How? Through our internal mind chatter, our intentions, our mirrors, our emotional pain body triggers, and through our perceptual filtered lenses.

Once you have become aware of something out of alignment, you can begin to clarify what it is and what the lesson is that your soul wants you to learn. You then can begin to heal and integrate the misaligned part into wholeness and alignment with your true essence.

How do we clarify what we have observed and become aware of, and how do we identify the lesson we are being taught? In most cases, the emotion you experience provides the answer.

I will reiterate the previous questions again, as these questions will help you identify the block, subconscious limiting belief, or trauma holding you back:

- What emotion did that trigger in me? And why?
- How did it make me feel? And why? This is your opportunity to bring the feelings to your conscious awareness
- How do I feel right now and why?
- What underlying belief do I have about life or myself triggered by this situation?
- How do I feel within myself right now?
- What is that deep feeling about myself that attracted this situation into my reality?
- What is the lesson my soul wants me to learn?

Here are a few scenarios, to allow us to apply the above questions:

A. I have been cheated on numerous times by all my partners, I feel deeply hurt. What is the subconscious belief that I might have about myself?

B. I am cheated on numerous times by all my partners, I feel deeply hurt, the deep emotion coming up for me is that I am never enough. What is the lesson?

C. I try and consciously manifest some money into my life, I don't get what I want, and I feel powerless. What is the lesson or subconscious belief I have about money?

D. My father consistently criticizes all my decisions, makes me feel like I am stupid and misunderstood. What is the lesson or belief that I have about myself?

E. I always feel like everyone is out to get me, like I have to live in constant fear that I will lose my job or my house. What is the lesson or subconscious belief?

So, let's work through this.

A. The belief is directly reflected here. You lack Self Love and your belief that you are not Enough or Worthy.

B. The lesson is directly reflected here. The lesson your soul wants you to learn is that you ARE ENOUGH. It can also be linked to Self-Love, and Self Worth.

C. The lesson your soul wants you to learn is that you are POWERFUL. But where do these thoughts reside? In the subconscious mind, and so there must also be a limiting belief of scarcity of money or abundance.

D. This one can get complicated. The lesson that your soul wants you to learn here can be a number of things, Self-Worth, block: Self Criticism, Self-Love, block: Self judgement, Self-Trust but also Validation and Approval.

E. The lesson your soul wants to learn is for you to move back into Love. Fear is the opposite of Love and Love is our natural state. If we trust God and we trust that God loves us why do, we fear? This lesson tells us to move back into Love, where we will not fear any outcome, we will know who we are, what we are, and we will be confident in that knowing. We trust that everything works out for our highest good. We are creators and so we can shift anything into a higher vibration. Let go of control and Surrender to the Higher Power within you. In addition, it will most likely also be a sub conscious belief that you are not safe and supported by the Universe, as a child most likely you didn't feel safe and supported by your parents or caretakers.

It does not matter whether you are able to get the correct lesson, as long as you are aware of the emotion beneath these triggers, perceptions and mirrors. These are all tools of Awareness to apply daily. And what this will do is expand your level of consciousness, allowing you to take responsibility over your creations and also giving your Power back to you, as it is yours. You are powerful beyond measure. You have created all this, and so you can change it.

Becoming aware of what is mirrored to you, what your perceptual filter is saying about yourself and what is triggered within your pain body, will tell you what it is that is not in alignment with who you are. Also by observing the underlying emotion or belief in someone else as to why they are getting triggered, how they might be seeing through their filtered lens and how we are too mirrors to them, can also allow one to see others with more compassion, love and awareness.

And this knowing can then allow you to begin to shift these illusions and limiting beliefs, healing all aspects and bringing it into wholeness. These tools of awareness give you the power. And these awareness's alone can be enough to already dismantle these illusions out from within your being. Yes! Just the awareness of it alone, can shift a mountain sized illusion.

STEP 6 - CONNECTING TO GOD-SOURCE

To begin healing, you must first connect to God-Source below and above you. You can only heal yourself from the position of the higher self, not the small self.

Before we come into this life, we are a part of a consciousness that many refer to as Creative Source or God. The terms do not so much matter as much as the understanding that we come from something that is greater than ourselves (the small self), to which we eventually return. Many of us know what it feels like to see ourselves as alone, disconnected, or separated. This is one of the biggest illusions of the material realm. As a Soul or beyond that, as Spirit, we are always connected to all of creation. Still that feeling of separation is one of the most painful that we will all come to know in this earthly realm.

Energy is needed for healing and it is important to connect with the right source for that energy. Our energy comes through our "prana tube," also known as our "life force energy. One must fully connect to the Source of all that is, our God Selves in order to create healing.

Why is it possible for certain healers including myself to instantly heal others emotional, physical and energetic blockages or ailments? This is because these individuals are already fully connected to the highest power which is God and they hold the space in order for healing to take place. And so it is not that only a few can heal, rather we all are healers, but in order to do this one must hold an extremely high multidimensional vibration as well as full inner knowing within us, in order for healing and expansion to be brought into reality. Just as many masters has done in past times.

So before I dive into how you can go about healing yourself, I will give you a step by step guideline on how to be fully connected to God Source, raising your vibration to love and above. To do our work here, one must be connected to God as God is the perfect thought form or essence which when visualized is then manifested into physical form. If we try and do this from the small self not fully connected to God Source, we can still manifest, but that manifestation is of a lower denser order. When Jesus said (John 10:30) I and my father are one, he was essentially saying that he was connected to the Source God Light, that him and God were one in the same. And this is what Christ or God Consciousness is.

Let's begin with an exercise now, and you can do this anytime. I would suggest doing this as often as possible:

Firstly, align your energy through prayer or meditation.

Now, I want you to look up 600 feet above you in your mind's eye, you are looking at God the source of everything, the omnipotent power of Love. Just look up and see/feel/sense/know the perfection of it.

Now you can image a golden column of light coming right down from above into your crown at the top of your head. All is of light and love.

Now also notice that there isn't any scarcity, lack, pain or suffering. In fact, everything is perfectly perfect and just absolute pure love. This is Bliss. There is only Love, abundance and joy everywhere.

Now, allow this feeling, this vision, this sense of God to come right into your own heart and soul. See, feel, know this divine blueprint of love to be your own, and in this instant know that the shift is happening within you.

Do this as often as possible.

STEP 7 - HEALING AND INTEGRATION

As you become more aware of your blocks, traumas, and subconscious limiting beliefs, you can begin to heal and integrate them—clear and replace them. In this section I will share tools and techniques you can use to instantly shift most of them; however, for deeper traumas and more deeply ingrained patterns, beliefs—whether personal or inherited—deeper shadow work will be needed. There are two healing modalities to use for the two types of emotional wounds. The first type of wound is subconscious limiting beliefs (personal or inherited). The second is trauma (parts of you that were formed in childhood that you suppressed, such as anxiety, fear, panic, anger, etc.).

7.1 Healing the Inner Child

You may have heard the term "inner child" and thought it was just another bit of psychobabble—even though the term has been around for many years now.

Your inner child is the echo of the child you once were.

We've been led to believe parenting is about fixing and producing our children. But parenting is really about raising ourselves. The child we must raise and heal first is the child within ourselves: our inner child. When we don't heal our inner child, we end up subconsciously projecting our unmet childhood needs onto our own children—which are the same childhood insecurities, doubts, and fears we work so hard to shield them from.

If we don't heal the wounds of our inner child, we can never experience the FULL, loving, and trusting connection we and our children both truly crave.

Healing our inner child is the heart of what conscious parenting is all about.

We each have our own history and we have all been influenced by our environment, events and the significant people around us. Our inner child has stored those memories, and their impact upon us.

Up to the age of six years, our brain was functioning at a relatively slow pace —the Theta brainwave frequency of 4-7 cycles per second— which is a very 'receptive' brainwave state, and we would have been profoundly affected by our experiences at that stage.

We will have made 'decisions' at a sub-conscious level, about how we 'should' be and what we 'should' do in order to be seen as okay, and to be allowed to stay around and to 'survive' within our families.

The mindset we form during that impressionable stage turns into the blueprint for what life "should" be. We carry our immature scripts and decisions with us into adulthood and they end up running our lives more than 95% of the time.

This is why we must revisit our childhood experiences to find out what our script says about our life and the unfolding drama we have been re-creating and repeating. Not doing so will result in playing out the same unexamined script and painful drama over and over again.

We cannot change the script by talking about it or by conscious effort alone. It was designed to keep us safe—albeit in ways that now hinder us—so it isn't going to give up that easily!

Most of the time we are living life like a child inside a grown-up's body - and the child within us yearns for attention, understanding, care and support.

We may try to silence these deeper longings with alcohol or drugs, by promiscuity, gambling, over-spending, over-eating, work-a-holism, self-harming and other ways of avoiding the real and deeper needs we have. Needs which we haven't allowed ourselves to become fully aware of, or to find a way to have sufficiently met.

Where does the inner child healing process begin?

We have all been influenced by our environments since the time we were in our mothers' wombs. The sounds around us, our mothers' stress levels, the abundance or deficit of the "feel-good" hormones and neuro-peptides, our nourishment or lack of it, complications, twin pregnancies, drugs, alcohol, and infections can play major parts in our sense of safety and security.

The actual birth experience, our early infant care, and the "emotional availability" of our mothers either reinforce or sooth the impact of those first pre-natal influences. As small children, we absorb a great deal from our extended families, our caregiver(s), friends, school influences, and religious institutions. We may not have had words for these experiences, but they are "logged" in our subconscious minds and bodies.

The aforementioned variables form a pool of experiences. In this pool resides our self-esteem, body-image, family traumas, shame and secrets (even unspoken ones, since all secrets affect the quality of caregiving). Most people's pools are a bit dirty; some people's pools are thick as mud. The dirtier your pool, the more wounds of your inner child.

Signs that your Inner Child is wounded

Take an honest look in the mirror. If you have any of these conditions, your pool is probably dirty. This is a long—but sadly not exhaustive—list:

- low self-esteem
- poor body-image
- mood and emotional imbalances
- problems with boundaries being too rigid or too weak
- problems with eating
- harming yourself
- psycho-sexual difficulties
- being "false" and wearing "masks," identity problems
- being a rebel or hoarder or bully or victim or super-achiever
- intimacy problems
- commitment problems
- a general lack of trust in yourself and others
- criminal behavior
- excessive lying
- being overly-responsible for others
- being fiercely competitive and a poor loser
- dependencies and addictions
- a lack of genuine friends
- obsessive and needy behavior
- fear of authority figures
- being manipulative
- being passive
- being aggressive.

These are the conditions that bring people to healing sessions, to repair and heal wounds caused by parents and others who didn't know any better. It is always about the unmet needs of the inner child: the place of both early wounding and most profound healing!

What can we do to help our wounded Inner Child?

You can learn how to meet, rescue, and "adopt" this wounded child who still lives deep inside you. After all, you are the only person who you can guarantee will never to leave you!

You can then emotionally contain and soothe your inner child and allow the competent adult inside of you to "tend to business'" out in the world. However, you must regularly stay connected with what your inner child still needs from you—which is, to be truly cared for by someone who wants the very best for them—that's you!

If you have a photograph of yourself as a small child, this will help you to empathically reconnect with him/her— the aim of which is to now understand their plight and to show them/yourself the compassion which has been missing.

It is often easier to feel compassion for other people than it is for yourself and you may have been rejecting and ignoring the yearning of your Inner Child - who has been calling out to you, over many years, for your interest, attention, compassion and love.

It may mean you now allowing yourself to have 'treats' and rewards that you would never have allowed yourself, or have been allowed by your parents, in the past.

The sensible competent Adult part of you should be able to set fair and sensible boundaries around this, so that you do not over-indulge yourself, or use any rewards as either a distraction or as a cover up for your deeper pain.

Rescuing and re-parenting your Inner Child will allow you to 'fill in the gaps' and enable you to live a more positive and rewarding life—with fun, laughter, spontaneity, authenticity, and most importantly, with love.

I want to heartily encourage you to re-parent yourself and your inner child by lovingly caring for her and by doing these things as often as you can (these apply to both boys and girls).

- Remind yourself how special and wonderful you were as a child
- Have a safe place that you can bring to mind where you and your inner child can meet and play together
- When you speak kindly to your inner child each day, have a loving and soothing inner voice – one that is supportive, soft, nurturing, patient and comforting
- Tell her/him she is now loved, valued, and appreciated by you
- Be sure to tell your inner little girl that she doesn't have to prove herself to anyone
- She has nothing to feel guilty or ashamed about. None of what happened to her was ever her fault. She didn't deserve to be treated badly.
- She was just in the wrong place and had no means of escape – but she is now free at last!
- There is nothing wrong with her/him. Tell them how proud you are of them
- She needs to feel respected. Don't tolerate disrespect ever again
- Tell her that you will be her guardian, champion and protector from now on. Things will be Okay and you will never let her come to any more harm
- She need never again fear being alone because you are always there for her now
- Apologize for not being aware of her pain and needs in the past, and of pushing her too hard sometimes to try and impress others

- Assure her that you will only allow safe, trustworthy and respectful people into your/her world now. Notice loving mothers who are caring for their babies and absorb that loving energy between a mother and child
- Reassure her that you will be alongside her either to speak up on her behalf, or to support her when she speaks up
- Agree upon a symbol of her freedom...something for her to summon up whenever she feels the need to escape and be alone with her thoughts. This might be (as some of my own clients have imagined) a ladder, a floating bubble, a sci-fi teleporter, a hot air balloon...anything that comes to mind that you/she can associate with release and freedom
- Regularly ask her how she's feeling and what she wants. Imagine sitting alongside that little girl, putting your arm around her shoulders and gently pulling her close to your heart.
- She has a home in your heart that she will never have to leave. She is safe with you now
- If she wants to cry let her cry and be there as her new mother to wipe her tears and soothe her pain or fear. Accept all her feelings and don't react negatively to what comes up. Be patient with her
- Remember that healing happens in different ways and timeframes. Promise to do your best to bring her the joy that has been missing from her life – and this will be profoundly healing for you both.
- Get back those things that brought you joy as a child – no matter how fleeting. Be sure to make a big thing of her birthdays and Christmas, holidays and achievements
- Set up creative activities for your playful inner child to enjoy! Bouncing, dancing, crafts, finger painting and anything else that takes her fancy. Drawing – from the right brain – is a great way to express your inner child's feelings. Allow doodling and unstructured drawing and see

what emerges when you're in the 'zone' of childlike creativity. Don't judge her efforts... just as you wouldn't judge a child bringing her artwork home from school to show you. Be proud and show it!

- Sing songs from childhood (whether you could sing well back then or not). Release any shame dumped on you for your singing ability - and instead enjoy stretching your vocal cords and making your own sounds that come from your heart and reach out into the world

- Encourage her to loosen up and allow physical and emotional intimacy (this will enhance your own sexual intimacy too). She must feel safe and unconditionally accepted to be able to do this. Show her that she can trust her own instincts and be guided by her own 'antennae' as to who is safe. She may doubt her ability based upon her mistakes in the past. You are healing now and as you grow in love for yourself and your life you won't want or allow anyone close to your inner child if they don't align with that self-love and a conscious caring relationship

- Whenever you have to leave your deliberate connection with her, always imagine placing her back inside the warmth and safety of your loving heart.

- Please remember that not only is your inner child a real part of your sub-conscious mind but also living in another dimension at this exact moment – a wounded child who needs your love, care and compassion...because no-one else can heal her pain and help her to make peace with the past.

Here Are 3 Steps to Healing the Inner Child

Doing these inner child exercises is a great addition or complement to any counselling or therapy that you may already be engaged in.

1. Access your inner child. Start by asking your inner child, how are you feeling right now? What would you like me to know? It may help to have a photograph of yourself as a child beside you.

You can make the space where you do this exercise inviting to your inner child by placing toys, teddy bears, or a children's blanket or night-light next to you.

2. Gain your inner child's trust. In truth, that part of you may have felt abandoned, betrayed, neglected, and forgotten by you, the adult self. You may need to take a little time to gain the trust of that part of your child self.

Much like you would in a conversation with a friend who is feeling vulnerable, reassure your child that it's safe to communicate.

At first your inner child may feel that they cannot trust you because they felt ignored or suppressed for so long. Reassuring the child (yourself) that you are now there for them will help the child feel safe. It's important that your inner child trusts your willingness to listen to, feel, see, or otherwise sense what they are experiencing.

3. Allow yourself to feel your inner child's feelings. Allow all of your feelings to rise to the surface. You may be surprised by what comes up when you first decide to say hello to that part of yourself. Expressing with the intention of releasing is so therapeutic.

There will probably be tears of sadness, hurt, shame, and anger. Crying is always a good release, and in a short while, you'll start feeling more compassionate toward yourself.

You may feel afraid that if you unleash your anger, you'll lose control. You won't. In fact, you'll have more control once you release the built-up energy of suppressed emotions. Without an outlet, those buried feelings always bubble up in ways that aren't pretty, so it's important to unearth them. Your subconscious mind won't give you more than you can handle.

7.2 Subconscious Limiting Beliefs

Every belief you have about people, life, relationships, religion, God, and so on—whether conscious or subconscious—was either taught to you, told to you, or based on subjective perceptions of your past experiences. Now, I'd like to pose a question for you to ponder: Just because something was told to you since you were young, does that make it true?

All of us absorbed many false beliefs when we were young, and those beliefs now limit us and cause pain. One of the problems with some forms of psychotherapy is that our programmed minds cannot heal our programmed minds. Much of our pain comes from the false beliefs that have been programmed into a part of our left brains called the "amygdala" (which is the seat of the ego, the wounded self). As long as we operate from the ego-driven wounded self, we will be stuck with those false beliefs. Why? Because the wounded self cannot heal the wounded self.

So how do we heal the false beliefs of the wounded self?

Healing occurs when we develop a part of ourselves. The loving Adult learns to take loving action in our own behalf based on the truth that is accessed from Spirit, and the more we take loving action for ourselves and with others, the more we heal the false beliefs that are limiting ourselves and causing our pain. In addition you can use the previous exercise when connecting to God-Source first to access the aspect of the Loving Adult/Higher Self.

While the wounded self always operates from an intent to control and receive love, avoid pain, and feel safe, the loving adult operates from an intent to learn about what loving ourselves and others truly means.

This shift in intent—from controlling love to learning about love— starts the healing process. There can be no deep, long-term healing as long as our intent is to control.

After healing our misguided intentions, we must also heal our misguided beliefs and make room for new beliefs. The mind has a lifetime of conditioned beliefs and expectations through which it filters all perceptions. While the body spontaneously lets go of pain the moment the underlying cause is healed, the mind has a mysterious instinct for holding on. Through the mind, we create a prison of suffering; we forget we are the architects of our own minds, and that we, ourselves, hold the key to our freedom.

What About Affirmations?

A major reason why affirmations don't work is if you create an internal battle with a deeply held negative core belief. Our core beliefs are the basis for our life. They effectively run our lives.

Saying an affirmation over a deeply held core belief can create inner conflict and, in the end, will only stress you out.

Instead of trying to stuff a positive affirmation in a very full box, try pull out the negative core belief. You can do this by asking questions about this core belief. Is it really true? Or is it something you inherited in your formative years? Is there any basis for this belief?

The chances are the answer is no because our beliefs are perceptions based on our worldview. So instead of ignoring your negative core belief, talk about it. Shed light on it. Bring it into your awareness and dive deep into uncovering it. When you realise that there is no real basis for it, you can begin to change this belief.

Often awareness alone is the tool that can transform your life, and then the affirmation is the catalyst to propel you forward or to replace the old core belief. Either way, affirmations shouldn't be used as a tool to disguise what's really going on.

Instead use them to assist you in leaping forward with your life and beliefs. But do the hard work if it is required, especially if you find some inner feeling that just won't shift. The best tool you can bring to this is awareness and begin to question it.

These words are like subtle thoughts and these thoughts act on your feelings. Your feelings then act on your belief system.

But you are unaware of all these subtle changes taking place.

Until one day you are in a fitting room, trying something on and you catch a glimpse of yourself in the mirror and you think to yourself; "WOW I am Beautiful!"

Or suddenly you begin to say, "Thank you!" to compliments instead of rejecting them. Or you do something that you never normally do, like putting yourself forward for something or going to a social gathering. You notice this small change in you. You don't know where it came from or how it happened. You can't honestly expect yourself to explode with confidence if you haven't felt good about yourself. Instead, watch for the subtlety. Take notice of the new good thought or feeling, no matter how small it is. By doing this, your good thought and feeling grows, until it becomes your new norm.

Begin to question all the subconscious beliefs that comes to the surface during the Awareness stages.

Ask yourself:

1. Is this really true?
2. Seek evidence to figure out if the belief is true.

3. Realize that your subconscious beliefs are mirrored in your external reality through others, through your circumstances and experiences. Look at how it is reflected back to you.
4. And then intentionally say the following words to release the old core belief:

"I now release the limiting belief or emotion [i.e. low self-worth] from my being now. I am releasing it in all dimensions from my past present and future, and I am releasing it to the Divine Source, to the highest vibration of love and light."

And as you release replace it with a new belief:

For example: "Replacing this now with Self Worth, and knowing my worth, replacing this with the knowing that I am enough and that I am powerful."

Yes, your intentions, your words, your statements and invocations are powerful when you are connected to the divine.

"We have to empty ourselves of everything. Period."

7.3 Shadow Work

The shadow is a psychological term for everything we can't see in ourselves. The personal shadow is the disowned self. This shadow self represents the parts of us we no longer claim to be our own, including inherent positive qualities.

These unexamined or disowned parts of our personality don't go anywhere. Although we deny them in our attempt to cast them out, we don't get rid of them.

What happens when you repress your shadow? What happens to all those parts of yourself that you sweep out of view?

We repress them; they are part of our subconscious. Think of the subconscious as everything we are not conscious of. So what Happens When You Repress Your Shadow? And what happens to all the parts of ourselves we sweep out of view?

Whatever qualities we deny in ourselves, we see in others. We call this "projection". We project onto others anything we bury within us.

If, for example, you get irritated when someone is angry at you, it's most likely that you haven't owned your own anger.

This doesn't mean the person isn't being angry towards you. However, if anger wasn't in your shadow self, someone else's anger wouldn't bother you so much. This process doesn't happen consciously. We aren't aware of our projections.

Our egos use this mechanism to defend itself—to defend how it perceives itself. Our false identities of being "good" keep us from connecting to our shadow.

The benefits of doing shadow work is obviously to heal, Un-become and master the self but it also benefits all areas of your life: It can improve your relationships immensely by changing your vibrational match to healthier people, partners, and situations. As you integrate your shadow side and come to terms with your darker half, you see yourself more clearly. You become more grounded, authentic, and whole.

When you can accept your own darker parts, it is easier to accept the shadow in others.

As a result, other people's behaviour won't trigger you as easily. Your previously filtered lens won't be filtered anymore. In seeing others and yourself as you are, you'll have a filter less lens with which to view the world.

As you integrate your shadow self, you're approaching your authentic self, which gives you a more realistic assessment of who you are.

STEPS ON HOW TO INTEGRATE THE SHADOW SELF?

Step 1: Choose something or someone to work on. It's often easier to begin with a person with whom you have difficulty (e.g., partner, relative, or boss) or even just an emotion that got triggered. My anxiety was severe and triggered constantly. I will use the example of my anxiety. When the feeling of panic set in, I couldn't breathe, swallow, or calm myself. The more I tried to remain calm, the more I panicked. I knew I had to work on my anxiety first because it controlled my life. How about you? Is there someone or something controlling your life? If yes, choose that thing or person to work on first.

Step 2: Face it: Now, from the perspective of your higher self, form an image of yourself or the person that triggered you and face it. Continuing with my anxiety example, I would form an image of my anxious self, looking so distressed, standing in front of me. Pay attention to all the details: their demeanour, they are wearing, and so forth. Now, look a bit deeper and identify what emotion is driving the condition. In my example of anxiety, it was fear. Whatever the emotion, feel it, embrace it, and welcome it. Try to understand it.

Step 3: Talk to it: Dialogue with this person in your imagination. If you are visualizing a person who triggered you, don't attempt to say the right thing. There is no need to be nice. The person you are describing will never see or hear this. Here are some guidelines:

Speak in the second person to the person. Or if it is an emotion such as anxiety, speak to the self you see in your mind's eye.

Speak directly to this person, as if he or she was there.

174

Ask questions such as: Why are you so angry, so sad, so anxious? What is it that you need from me? What are you trying to show me? What do you have to teach me? What is it that you needed from me or anyone else that you never got during your childhood? Imagine their responses to these questions. Speak the imaginary responses out loud. Record the conversation in your journal if you like.

Acknowledge that part of you.

Give it what he/she/it asks for.

Tell them how much you love them. Why? Because the person you see is you. That is, it is an aspect of you that disintegrated, that fractured off, that was denied or disowned. You can even imagine that this aspect of you hugs you, embraces you, and forgives you.

If this aspect of you is not ready to be integrated, to heal, that is okay. Thank them for being there, for trying to protect you. Continue to love and embrace this part of you.

Step 4: Be it: Now, if this aspect of you is ready, usher them into you and allow them to become whole with you again. You can do this with as many aspects of you as many times as you want.

Know that this is not your imagination. This aspect of you lives and whatever you shift during visualization, you are literally shifting and healing yourself, simultaneously in all other dimensions as well.

This process allows you to re-own and integrate shadow aspects into yourself, where they will no longer haunt and trigger you.

STEP 8 – CONSCIOUS CREATION

When you learn how to consciously create, you will learn how to manifest things into your reality. Conscious creation uses the law of attraction to create exactly what you want. Good or bad, you already create your reality, perfectly. You're currently creating your reality 100% of the time, flawlessly. You could not be a better creator if you tried. It's the way the universe works. Right now, your emotions, thoughts, and beliefs are creating your world every single moment. This system works whether you know it or not and whether you believe it or not. That's just the way it is.

The problem is, until you learn to create consciously, you're creating unconsciously. When you create unconsciously you probably won't be too happy because you will have no control over what you create. When you become conscious of your energy, you can learn to change the things in your life that you don't like.

You become empowered to literally create all the abundance and experiences—whatever it is you desire. How is this possible? Divinity.

Your body, this planet, and everything that happens outside of you is actually an illusion. The only real thing is the "you" beyond your body: the you who decided to have a physical experience on earth.

Why? To go on the learning adventure of remembering who you are (divinity personified) and for the fun of consciously creating your world.

Conscious creation is simply becoming conscious of what you think, feel, and believe, and directing your thoughts, choosing your emotions, and changing your beliefs so that they are in alignment with what you desire. It's not just you, the conscious "you," who has to be in alignment. The past "yous" must be in alignment also. Conscious creation is easy, but it is also complex. Conscious Creation is all about working deliberately with the spiritual tools you have in order to prompt more flow in your life, release energetic resistance and actively pursue alignment with the intentions that you desire to manifest.

176

HOWEVER, most beliefs and past conditioning were never taken on by conscious choice and were installed by default. Most of us that are still asleep, even those that are awake, are still running on autopilot. Where the subconscious is still running your lives.

There is therefore no logical reason why thoughts and beliefs should have so much power over us, nor any reason why we should be enslaved by them.

But once we begin to release those old subconscious beliefs and programming, one's existence becomes less of an unconscious prison and more a playground of transformation. And this is Creating Consciously, through intent, through desire with no limitations known or unknown.

Life is a process of remembering and creating more so than a process of discovery.

STEP 9 - SPIRITUAL MASTERY

Question everything. Period.

"Allow yourself to acknowledge that some of your old beliefs about God and about life are not true and are no longer working. Explore the possibility that there is something you do not fully understand about God and life. Believe that a new understanding will change everything. Announce that you are open and willing to gain new understandings of God and Life. Believe that new understandings could produce a new way of life on this planet. Courageously examine new understandings

and, if they align with your personal inner truth and knowing, enlarge your belief system to include them."

Riana Arendse

Mastery is about getting out of wanting and asking, but rather CHOOSING and BEING.

No matter how many times you are told what you "should" believe, there is no greater understanding than the intuition your own heart will provide. The student becomes the master when he or she realizes that everything they know, they already know deep inside of themselves. When the student's faith is in himself and the Divine Universe, he becomes the master.

The master always trusts his own wisdom above anyone else's, and the master also knows that he already knows everything he needs to know for that exact moment. He has faith that the minute more wisdom is needed, it will be provided by the Divine higher intelligence. Therefore, he doesn't strive constantly for more information. Period.

Below are the principles of Mastery I have used and still use in order to fully embody the truth of who I am, which is the truth of who we all are.

Principles of Spiritual Mastery:

- **Integrating Ego**

Spiritual mastery requires for the ego (separate sense of self or I) to be integrated. It is not to defeat your ego. It is not to disown or transcend your ego. It is to integrate your ego. To integrate your ego, you must really own it as part of yourself. You must see it, hear it, feel it and come to understand it so that you can meet its needs and care for its best interests. The ego needs to be integrated and brought into wholeness in order for you to be able to see reality AS IT IS, and not what your ego WANTS it to be. The lower aspect of your ego is based in illusion and deception → the opposite of self-awareness, which is based in truth.

- **Awareness and Clarity**

Self-awareness is the starting point on your spiritual path. By knowing who you are, you can achieve self-awareness. Awareness is the most exciting step because you get to explore and discover who you are. And awareness based on the steps in the Un-becoming process within this book, is vital in ones journey toward healing and mastery.

Through clarity of these awareness's, you have the ability to make better decisions that are more grounded and empowered, that are in alignment with your spirit.

- **Heal**

A Light heart is a Strong heart. Therefore, you need to heal any physical, emotional, or spiritual pain holding you back from being your greatest self. Masters knows how to identify these areas and how to heal themselves.

- **Commit to Truth**

To attain a state of Spiritual Mastery (and remain there long enough to be able to make use of the state) – one must be committed to the path of truth. All lies cause confusion and distract one from the true path. Lies, deceptions, illusion create effects that dampen one's vibration and keeps one trapped in a state of separation from Source / Ultimate Truth. For the Divine to be completely open with you – you must be open with it – lies create barriers and resistances to true intimacy with the Divine. Spiritual Truth cannot be perceived from any state not aligned to truth – and thus Spiritual Mastery is the product of a transmutation and disallowance of all lies!

- **Affirm and Declare who you truly are**

Spiritual masters know the truth of who they are, through the practice of self-definition, self-affirmation and self-declaration.

When you know who you are, no one can tell you who you are.

When you know who you are, you then embody this knowing. And this embodiment is true mastery..

Becoming your True Self requires holding less beliefs in mind – not more

STEP 10 – DECLARATION OF SOVEREIGNTY – (Channelled Text from the Ascended Masters)

Christ Consciousness

Many years later, upon my spiritual awakening, I met with the Teachings of the Christ. But this time around, they were presented to me in a very different form then previously taught through my earlier religion, and these new understandings offered me the revolution of my own heart that until then had remained firmly closed.

Firstly I became fully aware that God/Source was not separate from us but within us and within everything around us....that life itself is God. Period.

And then I realized that the Christ Teachings were not just words of wisdom but indeed pure consciousness; seeds of consciousness that we already carry inside and through the process of receiving both the new spiritual learnings and the practicing of meditation, this Christ Consciousness could simply grow and develop from within our own being, as a remembrance of all those magnificent Christ qualities of Light that are always present within us.

Despite the name, the fact of Christ Consciousness transcends Christianity, Hinduism, and every other religion. Paramhansa Yogananda explained that the Christ consciousness is the spiritual essence hidden at the core of each individual, in fact at the core of every atom of creation. Therefore, Jesus is not Christ, rather Jesus (the person) was the vessel for Christ Consciousness to express itself in the physical.

Simply put, Christ Consciousness is two main things. It is free will and it is love. If you put this together Christ Consciousness is quite simply the choice to love. And love is Oneness (recognizing oneself in all things).

To be awakened, to be conscious means to align our Consciousness with the Christ Consciousness as the evolution and growth inside our awareness simply signifies to fully accept and embrace all the Christ Principles as we inherently are.

Christ Consciousness is God's Infinite Intelligence that is present in all creation. The Infinite Christ is the "only begotten son" of God the Father, the only pure Reflection of Spirit in the created realm.

When you expand your identity from this body and personality to the omnipresent spirit, and raise your vibration to the highest octave, you realize your consciousness to be everywhere—all throughout the entire universe. Then you have attained "Christ Consciousness," just as Jesus and the other Masters have done before.

They are here now and would like to proceed with today's channelling:

Yes we are here...

Wherever you incarnate within this multiverse and vast tapestry of reality, we will assist you now in anchoring the radiant Christ light of your Higher Self through these invocations, initiations and commands that follow.

We say to you now that to truly embody your Christed Self is a journey that requires extraordinary courage to complete. A courage that we as the ascended masters have embodied and demonstrated for you in our own previous incarnations. As the collective voice of the ascended masters, we represent many who have gone before you and who are now Masters and Mentors assisting you on your own personal spiritual journey. You are most likely aware of a few of us as explained in this book, if not more, some would include the Christ, Mother Mary, Mary Magdalene, Buddah, Isis and Hathor to name a few. Some of you will encounter us along your journey and choose to work directly with us along this journey of embodiment you so willfully choose through your

182

sovereignty. And we could not be any happier and filled with unconditional love for you. As you are us and we are you.

It is our great joy to guide you along this pathway of accelerated embodiment, initiations and healing, returning back to the source within all of you.

As ascended masters we were also once human beings, as some of you may know. We were genetically operating with the fully activated divine power of Source. Our names and our spiritual leadership appears to most of mankind to be almost God-Like to those who are still asleep or unconscious to this same eternal and divine potential given to ALL. Yes we only embodied these in form and displayed these wonderful miraculous works as an example of who you are too, and what you too can do.

Humanity has since worshipped and praised us for the work we did, however this worship was never required nor desired. For our service as the ascended masters is to honor and reflect the sovereign master who already exists within you all.

You will discover if not already in this book, that you are God, Source, there is no one above or below you.

This allows you now to immediately shift into a state of peace in which you feel safe enough, to allow all others the same acknowledgement without reservation. That you are all Masters and you all have the divine inheritance awaiting you.

We say to you now that everything that humanity experiences, including all the suffering - as a physical reality is actually a hologram, a holographic illusion, a matrix. It is not truth. It is not real, however it can appear to be so, and it in no way diminishes humanity's experiences, for we too walked in your shoes before. We walked this path many a time.

And so we come to you now as loving witnesses, as you begin to accept this initiation by declaring your full sovereignty.

Your true nature is holy, is love, is joy and your true nature is peace.

Your true nature is the same essence, energy and creative power that birthed all that is, that birthed the stars and that birthed all of creation. That is your true nature, yes.

However, to fulfill your magnificent purpose here, you must relinquish small ideas and limiting beliefs about yourself and believe in who you truly are. So that you can create a new world.

It is safe now to stand in your sovereign Power as Source, as our presence is with you now as you make the following declaration and receive this initiation. Wait no longer for the divine inheritance that has been and is already yours.

Your Higher Self steps forward now to activate you.

Before you begin, imagine unconditional love now pouring in the top of your crown chakra, flowing down throughout your entire body, and within every cell.

All your energy bodies now align in preparation for releasing all past contracts, agreements, vows and oaths. Made in past lifetimes and in this.

Say out loud:

I call on my higher self to merge with me, guide me, and assist me in declaring, embodying, and enacting one hundred percent sovereignty of my being in this and every now moment, in alignment with my I Am Presence and in accordance with my chosen purpose, goals, and intentions for this lifetime. I call upon the elemental, angelic, ascended, cosmic, and ancestral realms to witness my declaration, to assist in upholding the integrity of its intention, and to co-create with me in manifesting my highest potentials personally, in unity with the one, and in service to the Earth as we graduate to the next level of our evolution. I now connect with my guides who have my best interest of freedom and sovereignty declaration in mind, and I gather my council of equity to review my contracts and agreements made in this lifetime as well as all lifetimes. I call up the agreements made that no longer serve me on a path to expansion and growth.

In declaring my full sovereignty and with the guidance of my higher self and I AM Presence, I assert autonomy over my physical and nonphysical embodiment, my energetic vibration, and all resulting emanations. I disallow any interference to distort or delay the fulfilment of my purpose in this lifetime—whether that interference be well-meaning, misguided, self-interested, or malevolent. This includes any and all overt and covert intentions, attempts, and actions to limit, separate, distract, manipulate, disempower, traumatize, dominate, control, or harvest any aspect or increment of my energy and consciousness. I state that I will no longer carry energy that is not of pure Source within me in this present moment and in any other moment as all aspects of me in the past, future and present are now to be healed. I fold space and time and go back to each time the negative or lower vibrational thought or energy was created, and I transmute it now to Source. My body is now cleared of any negative thought forms and energies that I created knowingly or unknowingly that had an intention of self-sabotage and negative emotion. I now heal my DNA and regenerate my body back to the organic template it was created to be.

I honor the Source of all that is, and bless the power of my free will, strength and ability to command wonders, to command change, to command release and to command healing, and to fulfill the divine will of my Highest God Self.

My Higher Self now prepares my body, mind and spirit in all dimensions for this full clearing now.

Hear the voice of your Higher Self now focusing your attention completely within your heart centre.

As a Sovereign Creator, of Source I now declare my full sovereignty. I now declare these invocations heard and answered.

Commanding now that every single Akashic record now be opened. Stepping forward now to witness all my previous incarnations and the beliefs, vows and contracts made then, to release all of them and rewrite them as directed by my Higher Self.

I ask my Higher Self to bless me with the courage and will power to authentically love myself.

I now guide my awareness to recognize and release the following beliefs:

I say this now through my divine right of commanding and willing.

Releasing now the inherited shame, guilt and rage accumulated in past lives and throughout all dimensions.

Releasing now the vows of poverty made in past lives and throughout all dimensions.

Releasing now the contracts made to keep myself small in all lifetimes and all dimensions.

Releasing now the fear that stepping into my Power will defy God. Releasing this now for I know who I truly am, as The Source.

Releasing now the fear of stepping into my true power, from all lifetimes and all dimensions.

Releasing now the belief that I am separate from God, throughout all lifetimes and dimensions.

Releasing now the belief that an external source controls my destiny. For I now declare the knowing that I am the creator and eternal source to my own life.

Releasing now the victimhood, blaming others and binding of my own eyes in seeing my true power.

I intend that in healing myself in this now moment, I heal other aspects of myself across time and space, as well as splintered aspects of other consciousness trapped in time who, through the domino effect, will attain the freedom to return to where they belong, to heal, and to contribute to the unity we seek to co create in order to graduate from this plane and take our next evolutionary steps. I offer healing, compassion, and forgiveness wherever it is needed or wanted to free all aspects of consciousness, including my own, to allow all to return to its natural order in wholeness and unity. I ask that this be entered into the earth Akashic record, so I have declared my I AM PRESENCE.

I am a holy human being and I am safe to now declare myself free of the bondage of all past lives to truly know and embody my sovereignty as a Divine Creator

I realize to embody my Sovereignty, I need to accept my true Divinity as the One, and that I am already Perfect, Pure and Divine.

I affirm this with all that I am, as Source

And so it is.

It is done.

It is done.

It is done.

CHAPTER 8:

You Are the Creator

Remembering who and what you are

Surrender the need to control what you know and understand about Source/God and about yourself. Release the need to feel comfortable in past conditioned and logical mind made beliefs and linear thinking. Open your hearts and mind to the inexpressible mysteries of Source, of You.

Who Are You?

God's promise to us is that we are equal to Him—nothing less and nothing more—and that we are responsible for our creations and for creating.

We are God and need to live as such. As God we can create heaven. But others of us will fear such changes that we may bring, and so they will stand against us. When accepting our truth, we will be accused, abandoned, and hated by them.

So why then pursue this goal? Why believe and remember?

Because we are no longer concerned with the acceptance or approval of the world; and because we seek a better world. A new Earth.

You are the Creator.

Period

You try to hold a consistent set of thoughts and concepts in your mind, but you cling tightly to these concepts. You define yourself based on what you believe. But it is not who you are. It is just the culmination of thoughts you have pulled around yourself in an attempt to define yourself.

But it is not who you are?

But then who are you? You are the Creator, yes you are God. To some who are not ready to receive this or remember this, this will appear as blasphemous or egoic. But I say to you: go forth and experience yourself as creator, for that is what you are and what you do.

Sai Baba said it so beautifully when asked the question "do you think you are God?" He replied, "Yes I am God, but so are you. The only difference is that I am aware of it and you are not."

And so many enlightened beings that came before, such as Jesus, Buddha etc. all had this knowing and embodied this knowing. Teaching us that we too are like them, we are all one. We are God/Source. We are Eternal. Period.

So, I pose the question again, do you know who you are?

Do you know who this is that is peering through your eyes and standing in your shoes?

God, not in the traditional way or use of the word, but a flowing river, consciousness of love that flows within all of us. It is your very essence. Period.

To many, the statement "I am God" rings of blasphemy. God, according to conventional religion, is the supreme deity, the almighty eternal omniscient creator. How can any lowly human being claim that he or she is God? Their inner explorations have revealed the true nature of the self, and it is this that they identify with God. They are claiming that the essence of self, the sense of "I am" without any personal attributes, is God. This concept of God is not of a separate superior being, existing in some other realm, overlooking human

190

affairs and loving or judging us according to our deeds. God is in each and every one of us, the most intimate and undeniable aspect of ourselves. God is the light of consciousness that shines in every mind. God is life itself.

God is everything and God is nothing all simultaneously. So, when we say we create our lives, we create it based on the law of attraction, the law of resonance. We do so for the most part from the small egoic, conditioned self. And so, if we are able to create everything we see in our external reality, this means we can change them as well.

We literally have the power to create all that which we desire, when we Un-become and when we align vibrationally to that which we desire. When we remove everything that isn't true—that isn't love— Completely within us, if we just listen and open ourselves up to experiencing our divine nature. If you could imagine God/Source as a star, and this star completely shatters or explodes into a million different pieces within the universe, these pieces are each of us. And so, we are in essence an aspect of the Source itself.

One's direct communication with God-Source, will always come through the experiences we have—not necessarily what we have been told through and by others, but through what we have felt and experienced within ourselves in relation to God. What do your life experiences perpetuate over and over? What is the message God wants to tell you? These are your experiences. Period.

God created you in his image and likeness, what does this mean?

When I received this information, a remembering of the truth, I realized who it was that was actually standing in my shoes, looking through my eyes, inhabiting this body. If God has created me in his likeness, in his image, that means I am a creator too, I am made of the same essence that God is, there is no separation only Oneness. And so, I have created everything in my life, because of the power God has given me when I incarnated on this earth. As a being on this earth I have been given free will to do as I wish to choose as I wish. Whatever truth I hold within my being—within my mind, my subconscious—is my reality, my creation, and thus what I believe it to be.

The truth is, there is only really love and fear. As humans we are constantly living in fear. How do I know this? Because if we lived in love, we would not need to worry about so many things. Rather, we would have a faith that is indestructible, and we would know the power that is inherent within us. All this tells me that we have lost our connection to the Source of all that is... and that is love... as a state of being.

If you have believed you are separate from God/Universe/Source/Divine, you have created a world that exists in separation instead of oneness. Now that that is beginning to be released, the structures that have been created to keep you from God in fear, out of alignment, are now being undone. And this will bring forth to you, liberation.

Do you know who and what you are? I ask this again: Do you know who you are?

Most of us live in fear. When it comes to relationships, to love, we are unaware that we can be abundant in all aspects of our lives. We do not trust; we do not know who we are.

If you really knew who you are and believed that with all your might, can you imagine the different choices one would make?

Imagine you have created everything you have ever experienced in life. Wouldn't it be liberating to know that you've used your power to create your life as it is, and through Un-becoming, knowing, and remembering you also have the power to un-create or change it?

Every decision that has ever been made by oneself, by society, by groups and countries, was either made out of fear or love. Period.

The reason I speak of Un-becoming as a practice, and as a journey of healing and unfolding, is because you must get in the practice of unlearning everything you have been conditioned to believe. Every trauma and every negative experience has shaped certain beliefs into our subconscious.

To truly realize your God-embodied self, you must Un-become the illusion and the untruth of everything. It is all about Un-becoming. It is an Un-becoming.

Your pain and suffering will eventually lead you to crossroads and turning points. The more you resist Un-becoming, the more you will suffer. You have the choice to choose a different thought, a different path. Do you not want to experience the brilliance of who you truly are? The power of true love? If you have picked up this book, you are called to it, you are a vibrational match to it right now. This is truth. Period.

You came here to create and recreate yourself over and over, to expand into the fullness of who you are. To define yourself as your highest intention and to experience your divinity, to experience your creations. To know yourselves and experience yourselves as God Source embodied as you. That is your purpose.

When we incarnated as beings on the earth, the whole purpose was for us to experience our creations and our innate power as Creator embodied as us. And so, in order for us to know our magnificence, we must also know the opposite of it. In order to experience our light, we must also know the dark. In order for us to know Love, and truly experience love, we must come to know fear. And this is where polarity comes into play.

Each and every event and situation is created and called in, by yourself for yourself, so that you can experience who you truly are. Period.

Life can show up no other way for you, than that way in which you think and believe it will. Whatever you believe to be, will be. Period.

What you fear most, is what will most plague and pester you – this is the universal law of attraction. As God/Source we have created this reality in order for us to know and experience ourselves as God – through experience and creation. In the past, Masters chose only love, in every moment, with every decision even as they were being killed, they still loved their perpetrators. As they knew they were one with the Highest Power and Highest Love. And that there is a divine purpose behind everything.

How can you get from here to where you want to be? How can you live as Source/God/ Divine embodied as you?

By seeking, by choosing, by consciously making the choice to live from love each day. To make the choice to live from our higher selves instead of the small separate sense of self.

95% of the time we are caught up in the illusion of separateness, of ego. And we live from the mind instead of the soul. Christ did it amongst other masters, so we say to you now, go and live like Christ each and every moment you are here. This is what we call Christ Consciousness – Christ represented who we all truly are, he was a reminder and example for us to remember who we are. He was the living expression of experiencing our God Selves embodied in form. Be present, be here, now. Leave past experiences as they were, create the new by remaining in your natural state of pure Love. Seeing yourself in all things. Separation is just an illusion.

First comes awareness, then self-mastery. You will know when you are on your way to mastery when you begin to see the gap

closing between your intentions and the manifestation and
creation of your intentions into your reality.

(Channelled Text from the Ascended Masters)

Today the ascended masters will be speaking through me. Know that you have created this for yourself. And these are truths you manifested in order to remember.

This book has arrived in your life through no coincidence. You may not know that now, but when you finished with your experience you will know this absolutely. This is what your soul has been yearning for. For some of you this will be the next steps to claiming yourself as the one true self, God. And for others it will be your awakening.

Yes we are here, we speak to you today to say but a few words. Words or rather remembrances as it were, for you to be activated with this already inner knowing of who and what you are.

And as we speak through Riana, she is unaware that it is actually her that is speaking, and it is actually all of you who is also speaking through her. As you are us and we are you. There is only one. The God that you know of is you, is us.

As discussed in this book, yes everyone is your mirror, you do live in a world where the law of attraction is in place.

The reason for your existence in this life, in all lives that you have lived, will live and are living, is purely for you to experience yourself as the creator, creating.

You have prior to your incarnation here, decided what it is you would like to experience, you have made contracts with others in order for these desires to be fulfilled. You have created all that you see and have experienced, even though it may have been on a subconscious level.

Your manifestations or creations will follow your idea about yourself. In simpler words, what you create is merely based on the template or idea you have about life, about yourself.

As God we have sent you, all of you into physical form, that God might know itself experientially as all that God knows itself conceptually. And this exists for you the same, as you are God. You experience that we are one, yet you choose not to believe this.

Now you might think that we have created you, but we tell you now that you are creating God. Recreating God anew over and over again. This is our very reason for being.

You are splendid. Do you know that?

Now we say to you, proclaim the divinity of who and what you are. If you deny yourself you are denying God. Jesus was one example of claiming his divinity as being one with God. He did so publically, as his intention was to be an example of who we all truly are.

The change you seek within your own individual lives and within your world, can only come through one way. Firstly by *BEING* who you truly are.

First we want to reiterate what has been said in this book. And that is that none of what you are experiencing is real. It is an illusion. And you are the magician. The Creator.

Now man has distorted many things about us, about God, as you have discovered or will be remembering. And want to tell you all that we love you, just as you are. There can be no other way. We love all of you equally, the so called innocent, the rapist, the murderer and the beggar.

196

And you might be thinking but why? Why would you allow people to be murdered and still love them for doing these heinous acts? We tell you now, nobody does anything inappropriate, and there are no rights or wrongs on the level of the absolute. As there is only a person with their own internal model of the world.

Riana spoke of her perpetrators and forgiving them, seeing the gift inherent in all that she has experienced. And so prior to your incarnation, you too have made contracts with other souls, for them to play a role or a part in this journey here on earth, in order for you to experience a specific desire.

For example, Riana had soul contracts with her perpetrators, they agreed to play that role as for her to experience the polarized aspect of what she came here to experience. Which would be for her to experience an aspect of her divinity as God. Riana trusted the process, and remembered who she is.

Nothing that has happened, has happened out of her knowing or creation. Know and understand that you are bringing it to yourself. Even though from your forgetfulness of who you are, your experiences in the realm of relativity, it might feel wrong or negative. But this is what you have called unto yourself, for divine reasoning. There is inherent perfection in everything that happens. Within your life and within the world that you see.

We are all at cause in creating the events of our lives, producing each of the circumstances we have and are experiencing. This may be difficult for some people to swallow, but it is the truth. There are no villains, no evil monsters, no wrongs or rights, there just is. No person does anything wrong given their model of the world. The secret of understanding is knowing that there is a purpose behind all events.

The world will bring you circumstances according to your filter or view, and only you can decide what those circumstances mean. See the glory of the process in the midst of the perceived tragedy. Now this might sound like an impossible thing to do, but when you move into Christ Consciousness, this will be easier. As you will see the gift and blessing in all.

Now we will speak more on the topic of time. As Riana has mentioned there is no time, the past as you know it and future is all happening right now.

And one of the secrets to healing is that, nothing you see is real. It is based on your imagination on your perceptual filter. And with this imagination, you can create anything. Hence all past healing is done through the imagination. Going back in the mind's eye to heal the inner child or to change an event and how you perceived or processed it, can be done through imagination or visualization. You have created it and so you can change it. Yes.

And I know that even if you remember the exquisite reason for your very existence, you do not seem to know how to get there from where you are. Walking this path and getting to a point of mastery, requires you to choose to claim yourself as God every moment of every day. And we say to you begin to see yourself as you truly are.

You want to be the God that you are, or the Christ that you are, begin by acting like it. Make choices in alignment with this. Each of you have own construction of God, your own way that you have created God. And as you begin to remember and grow, you will recreate this construction of God as you.

The events which have occurred for the last few thousand years, is yet a reflection of the collective consciousness of the whole group on earth. We create what we believe.

We would like to touch on the next subject now. Mastery.

When you begin to move into a state of mastery, you will be aware of so many things. That everyone creates their realities and everyone is on their own journey of experiencing themselves as God.

There are obviously people in dire need of help in your world, but it is also true that at a very high level, no one is disadvantaged or a state of negativity. For each soul creates for itself the exact people, events and circumstances needed to accomplish what it wishes to accomplish.

You choose your parents, your country of birth, and all that comes with it. Similarly throughout the days of your life you continue to choose and create more of this to bring you the perfect opportunities you now desire in order to know yourself as you truly are. And you might ask, but does that mean I must ignore the man who has no food, the people who live in poverty, the woman who got raped. The countries that are suffering.

And we say to you, that is a very good question.

On the level of mastery, there will be only one question to ask yourself when encountering such an opportunity to help. And that is, firstly decide who you want to be, and how you want to create yourself as. You are creating yourself anew in every moment. For that is your purpose. Stretching your consciousness to unlimited heights. Ask yourself, who am I and who do I choose to be in relationship to this? What do I want here? Sometimes the best way to love someone or help someone is to leave them alone, or empower them, be an ear or give them advice, or teach them to empower themselves.

Sometimes it is extending help to them. But the best help you can give anyone, is by reminding them of who they truly are. Honor where others choose to be. This is the way of all the great masters, those who have walked this path before. When your help is offered in such a way that it creates continued dependency rather than independence then it would not be in their best interest. Make every choice based on your true inner knowing at that exact moment.

We love you

(Channelled Text continued)

When you raise your vibration to the highest you are in accordance with God as that, as the Creator. As we have said before, at the deepest and highest level you are the Creator, as we are. We are you and you are us. And so we want to talk about claiming yourself as such, as the Creator in form.

Know that the name you have chosen for this life is only but a tag or identity you have chosen for this life, however this is not the identity of your soul.

The true essence of your soul must be claimed. And so as you claim yourself as the Creator, you immediately begin raising your vibration or frequency so you call it, and then your journey will begin to unfold quickly.

Why is it important to claim yourself as the Creator?

For that is the truth of who you are, and until such time that you claim this, you will continue to limit yourself of the magnitude of who and what you are.

When you claim it you begin to integrate it, you then begin to claim it in thought, in word and deed. You then begin to claim it in relation to others and this gives them also permission to claim their divinity as the Creator too.

When you claim yourself as the Creator the Source of all, you begin to align yourself to a higher knowing and higher consciousness. When you access God's highest wisdom, you are in essence accessing your own. You have seen many examples before and now, masters as such,
200

who operate from their inner knowing and not from the confines of what they have been taught to believe.

This proclamation will eventually become knowing. And to be in the knowing of something, means to be presently in truth. That what you are claiming is truth.

This book is not telling you what to do or where to go, rather that you have the knowing inside of you already. The deeper truth of everything, that is already inherent within yourself. This books main purpose is not to add new information or beliefs to your mind or to try convince you of anything, but to bring about a shift in consciousness, that is to say, to awaken you. This book can only awaken those who are ready. Not everyone is ready yet but many are, and with each new person who awakens, the force within the collective consciousness grows to a higher octave.

But we want to tell you also this, If you want to embark on this path of knowing and mastery of your true self, and continue to release and heal all that no longer serves you, you can create this healing now in manifestation, you can ask for it now.

And to the degree that you are willing to open these floodgates to heal yourself, or to begin to Un-become, you will manifest this. If you so choose this, you are going to have to unblock or remove the mechanisms in place that prevents you from moving forward and healing yourself. You can do this quite easily now.

So we ask you this:

Would you now be willing to align yourself to the possibility of recreating yourself to the highest light of consciousness? And anything that stands in the way of your full healing to now be cleared completely now in safety, in love and in absolute peace?

If you affirm this, you set into motion the passage of energy release and beliefs that is required to bring this into manifestation.

I AM THAT I AM

I CLAIM MYSELF AS THAT I AM

I AM THAT I AM THROUGH INTENTION

THROUGH THOUGHT, WORD AND DEED

I AM

CHAPTER 9:

The Rising of a New Consciousness

Un-becoming and embodying your Divine essence

Embodiment is a time of reconciliation and integration, of all disconnected parts and this arises within the understanding that all is one great whole that everyone and everything is made up of the very same energy, Source. An integration of our shadow parts and light parts. Welcoming each and every part of ourselves with LOVE.

With this knowing, comes the ability and desire to bring all aspects of self that feel separated, back home. This includes how one views the world. It is a love affair with all of oneself, knowing nothing to be separate, in truth.

Believing in time—a past and future—is characteristic of living with a separate sense of self. From that perspective, the spiritual journey proceeds until eventually, at some point, inner integration takes place and light and dark are unified into a single whole again.

It is just the divine serving itself. That's it.

A shift in consciousness is the movement from one level of conscious awareness to another. As you go forth on this journey of awakening, healing, integration, and self-mastery, your consciousness will expand. The more you Un-become, the more you can begin to embody your true, divine essence—that which is truly you.

We are operating as only partially conscious beings due to our conditioned minds as well as an obsession with our more basic desires (preoccupation with the physical experience and its pain, suffering, desire, and temporariness).

Simply put, rising to a new Consciousness, once installed and fully activated, will remove "the box" of limitations that currently dictate your expectations. It will allow you to dream and realize dreams your logical mind currently does not allow.

This Higher Consciousness changes all the rules. In fact, there would be no rules. Rules are made by you, whatever you resign yourself to, tell yourself, believe to be true, will be.

And so, from a higher perspective you ARE the CREATOR of all of this.

Most of us are in a state of sleep even when awake, meaning we are blind to the true nature of existence. But it doesn't have to be that way. Awakening to the truth of you will allow you to see the illusions and give you the capability to consciously be conscious or consciously be unconscious.

We see what we perceive to be reality, but only through the unconscious lenses of our past conditioning (which is completely different from others' past conditioning). That means that for every single person alive today, there is a different reality, a different truth.

Awakening is just the beginning. The embodiment of awakening is the real journey. Authentic awakening is not static; it's a fresh moment-to-moment awareness of truths unfolding within our direct experience. It's not about "spiritual practice." It's not something we do for 10 minutes twice a day and then go back to our mind-made story life. Rather, it's a 24-7 job that calls us to be ruthlessly honest. You either meet life consciously—awakening to your true nature—or you get lost in the sleep state or unconscious life.

There's no half-way point. Why? Because every time something feels good, or you get things to go your way, it will all go wrong or hurt, and you'll get lost in your mind-made story again. Fortunately, you can become aware of what is still unconscious in you.

204

If awakening is to be complete in you, it must become alive in every cell of your being.

"Our deeper understanding tells us that a truly evolved being is one that values others more than it values itself, however this is far from the truth. Oneness is the ultimate truth, and this means that in essence we are all one and in the same. There is no separation. Therefore self-love is indicative of one who is truly evolved. What you do for yourself you are doing for another. When you love another as a part of you, there is no separation. By reflecting upon this truth and the expanded understanding of evolution, one that validates our deepest truths, we can see the love inherent in this."

Riana Arendse

Embodiment

Embodied spirituality is the practice of not only having the knowledge and understanding truths with your mind, but also anchoring them into your human being. Embodiment makes truth a practical, lived, and spiritual experience within your physical reality.

It's something I had to learn the hard way.

And in order to get to a sustainable point of embodying your true nature, one must empty itself of everything that is untrue. This is the un-becoming part.

To truly Un-become means that everything that is unconscious in you will be brought to the fire of awakeness to be transformed. That 95%

of your shadow of your subconscious must be made known to you and released.

Fittingly, it is during the process of healing and Un-becoming when confusion, doubt, and fear surface. At that point, you might think, "Surely if I'm enlightened or healing or Un-becoming, I shouldn't be having these negative thoughts or painful feelings?"

It's at this point that there's a danger of re-identification with the mind made story of your life. And it's exactly here that the invitation to the greatest opportunity, holds out its hand to you. Right here, in this moment - and in each moment as it unfolds, whether it be an enlightened or an unenlightened moment - you are invited to rest more deeply within the One that expresses itself as everything, your inner being, your divine self.

You are invited to willingly open to the divine mystery and mess of what we call the human experience. If you choose to be unequivocal in taking up this invitation, remember there is no half-way point. Once you accept the invitation, your life will no longer be your own but rather in service to your new journey to awakeness. If you are sincere and committed in your surrender to awakeness, the light of your innermost being will come rushing to meet your outermost expression, and everything that stands in the way of this truth will be destroyed.

Either way, if the destruction job is thorough, an incredible stillness will emanate from your core and reverberate through your world. This stillness is your true power because it is inseparable from the silent core of creation. It is the light of Source.

The embodiment of this light is the start of authentic living and oneness.

206

Oneness

Oneness is an experience that transcends the mind. When we experience oneness, we feel a connection with everything in existence on every level. In other words, we feel 'at one' with all things.

It is the feeling of fullness, vastness, and completion. It is the experience of embodying our true nature, the Self that exists beyond our limited personas.

Oneness is your birth right; it is the true nature of reality. In other words, not only do you have the right to experience it, but it is an integral part of your destiny as a spiritual seeker.

When life is broken down into thoughts, concepts, ideas, and beliefs, we cannot directly experience the Oneness of everything. Instead, we perceive life through a broken filtered lens. Until we can take off those filtered lenses, we will continue to see ourselves as isolated and separate.

Because our minds dominate so much of our lives, we also tend to feel internally fragmented and disintegrated. The nature of the mind is to seek understanding and safety. And in order to understand life and be safe, we must see some things as 'good or positive' and some things as 'bad or negative.' Splitting life into good/bad and right/wrong is a very natural process because it helps us to survive. But at the same time, splitting life into polarities or opposites also creates tremendous suffering in us.

How does polarity create tremendous suffering?

Because we grow up learning that some parts of us are 'good' while other parts of us are 'bad.' We then attach to the 'good' parts of ourselves, (as we have been taught and conditioned what is acceptable), and then we repress or deny the 'bad' parts of ourselves.

What happens when we start to perceive ourselves in a fragmented way? The answer is that we feel fractured, lacking, not good enough, and incomplete. We start to feel insecure, anxious, lonely, depressed, and in some extreme cases suicidal. Our essence has been diluted. We feel fake and inauthentic. Emptiness haunts us. And while we greatly crave to love and embrace ourselves, we can't—because we love some parts of ourselves and hate the others. This is why integration is so important. Integration is the opposite of fragmentation. When we integrate, we unite different parts of ourselves which may have been missing for years or decades. When we seek integration, we are seeking oneness.

To have more than a fleeting glimpse of oneness, you must make the unconscious conscious. When you embrace both your humanity and divinity, you can experience self-compassion and self-acceptance. These qualities and practices are essential on the spiritual path. Without learning to love ourselves in all our weirdness and wildness, it's impossible to fully open to the experience of oneness.

Returning To Love

"The potential we have as human beings, when we tune into the heart frequency, and operate completely from a space of multidimensional love and compassion – is the ultimate level of transformation and consciousness. Love is truth, and to live from truth IS our natural essence."

Riana Arendse

When we don't allow others to see all aspects of us, all of our parts, we are in turn living from the illusion of separation. But when we are living authentically sharing all aspects of us dark and light, we are living from the view of Oneness. That we all are one. And this is true on a Universal basis. We fail to see that everyone we come across are indeed our mirrors, we are one in the same.

How can this be true that everyone is my mirror? I do not hurt, I do not have anger, I did not create how other people treat me, I am the victim.

Yes, this is what you may firmly believe today—but only from a conditioned perspective. When you come to realize that on an energetic level you cannot attract into your reality what isn't already a match to a frequency or vibration within you, you will begin to take responsibility for your life. In addition when you come to realize that you have agreed to all of this prior to your incarnation, and that everything you have experienced is perfectly divine and just as it should be, you will begin to step into your true power and remembrance of who you truly are.

To be truly free, we must rid ourselves of our mind-made stories and beliefs. Why? Because we are not our story, we are so much more.

Living the illusion that we are just victims is just an attempt to feel even more powerless. Victimhood robs us of our true divinity. When we realize that people that harm us are also only victims of victims, we can begin to forgive and see them through the eyes of God, of the Divine, embodied as each of us.

Most of us operate out of fear. It dominates every aspect of our beings. We fear death, loss, sickness, scarcity, insecurity, and not being enough, to name a few. Like it or not, these fears are often running on autopilot, directing our lives. Where do most of our fears come from? Mainly past experiences. Fear-based thoughts usually occur when our attention is fixed on the past and future instead of the present. We create fearful situations into our lives because we consciously and subconsciously focus on them. The present moment is all there is, and it is where your attention needs to be most of the time.

The only way to move from fear to love, is to embrace fear. It is to meet fear with Love.

When most of us experience fear, we try to push it away with our minds. Instead, we need to face it, fight it, re-frame it, judge it, and shame it, all of which will invite a spirit of acceptance.

When I'm afraid, I take it as a sign that I have tuned out of my Soul mind, so to speak, and I'm now listening to Ego inside my head. It's time to re-attune oneself back into love. And so, in a moment of fear, ask yourself, what would Love do, what would Jesus do, what would God do?

A quote to ponder by Helen Schucman in the book A Course in Miracles: "The presence of fear is a sure sign that you are trusting in your own strength."

Trusting in your own strength meaning in the small self, not the true Self. Most ego's default position is self-reliance. This old habit fences

210

one off from people and from the Divine's help. But when we realize that Source God has no limitations, and that we can rely on the power of Source God within us, we move away from trying to do things as the small self, and are in the knowing that our higher power can take the reins. Meeting fear with love helps us to let go of stories and experience true reality.

The spiritual journey involves giving up fear and accepting love. When we give up being fearful and weak, we become loving and strong. We accept that the power of the universe, of Source God is within us, as us. We practice forgiveness. And we become generous.

Mark Twain said it well when he quipped, "I have been through some terrible things in my life, some of which actually happened."

Think about all the times we would worry about the future or are afraid that just around the corner our lives would fall apart. About all the times we would fear an outcome based on past experiences. Yet 95% of those fears never happen. And fear in essence, is contraction, it is resistance. And whatever resists persists.

Listening to fear does not mean you have to live your life at the mercy of fear; but rather welcome it. Just because you have an emotion of fear does not mean you have to act on that emotion. You simply have an opportunity to become aware, question and seriously consider the emotion of fear. And return back to Love, which is the only truth.

Right now, you have 1,300 potentials for tomorrow, but your path forward depends on only one thing: how much you love yourself today, and nothing else. Why? Because when you are in a vibration of unconditional self-love, you are inhabiting the highest, most powerful frequency in the multiverse.

The truth is, what and who you attract tomorrow will be vibrationally matched to what you are holding in your being today. Are you holding fear or love? Are you emitting fear or love? Are you expressing fear or love? You will know the answers to these questions tomorrow.

Your present is literally creating potential for tomorrow. And you have the ability to shift it to what you desire. Period.

Ones Commitment to Un-Becoming

"You can only lose what is not real, what is untruth."

Riana Arendse

Some of you many wonder how I figured all of this out since it is deep and requires a lot of processing and understanding.

After I learned the truth of who we are and how we create our realities, I committed myself to healing and shedding all that wasn't truth. I placed my full trust in the Universe/God. I was extremely committed to it, because I knew my purpose was in the journey of unfolding. So, I faced my pain, I processed it, I tried different things to heal myself, and through trial and error (and my gifts opening), I managed to heal all my blocks and limiting beliefs. I had to do it on my own to step into my purpose of being a teacher and healer.

That said, this journey is not for the faint-hearted. It takes commitment and dedication, period.

As I said earlier, I made my mind up early on that learning the truth was more important to me than any old comfortable illusion. I welcomed issues and trying moments, because I knew they were opportunities for me to heal even more. When I healed one thing I would say, "Okay universe, what's next? I'm ready." I was committed. Why? Because I couldn't go back to living a lie, an illusion, anymore. I could never return to feeling like a victim, like everything was happening to me. Upon discovering the truth that I was more

212

powerful than I could ever imagine, I became fully committed to Un-becoming, learning, and living it.

If you've had your spiritual awakening or dark night of the soul, do you ever feel all over the place? Lost and confused? Not knowing where or how to start?

I've felt lost and confused in the beginning and in many other parts of the journey. Initially, I did everything in my power to change my reality through action and healing, yet nothing got better. I had to learn to surrender and give up control. I was still trying to hold on to the wheel out of fear. From that point of awareness forward, whenever I tried to take control of the wheel or attach myself to an outcome, I would just tell myself, "Riana, let your higher essence decide for you, let the higher power take over." Things only started to shift when I really surrendered. I also had to remember that that higher power was already me, and not anything outside of me.

The above statement also applies to the previous teaching about the necessity of surrendering to the flow of Divine love.

Just as you cannot have 1 foot in the door and 1 outside of the door, ones' commitment to Un-becoming on this spiritual path is vital. For most of us we tend to not want to fully let go of the illusion we have been living. Living in fear, afraid to let go of control. Our sense of separation, our conditioning, our ego becomes way too dominant for us to fully commit to this path. To reiterate, Un-becoming is not a journey to become something enlightened or more spiritual, to actualize gifts and abilities, or to achieve abundance; rather, it is a transformative journey to shift us from small self to higher self.

We came here to enjoy our human existence for the short time we will be here, and yet we live in so much untruth, so much suffering. I remember when I embarked on this journey, I made a complete commitment to healing and Un-becoming, because the truth for me was more important than any temporary feeling of comfortableness, familiarity or happiness. I wanted to live as I truly am as a Creator and it didn't matter what loss, heartache and pain I needed to face in order to Un-become. I was willing, I was surrendered in all my glory.

During my healing journey I lost my job, my nine-year relationship ended, and I was in pain and grieving. At the same time, I asked God/Universe, "Okay, so what's the next part I still need to heal?" I was eager and excited to heal the next block and the next block. But even this was a part of my ego and separate self; I was still striving to be something better. This too I had to surrender and just let go and trust.

For most people, the driving force behind fully committing to Un-becoming is usually a build-up of severe pain and suffering in which one's darkest moment becomes the catalyst for expansion, growth, and enlightenment. It is the point when a person is fully brought to their knees for the 100th time and decide they are done with living the way they've been living. This is the moment where commitment to healing, to Un-becoming, really takes form.

For other, sometimes it takes a bit more than that to get to a point of no return. Either way, the glorious point of no return is the moment one can truly commit, truly surrender, and truly allow the divine flow of love to sweep in and take over. It is the moment one gives rise to higher consciousness. It is the moment one no longer identifies with the small self but surrenders to the flow of universal love and higher self. It is the moment of truth.

Following the world's commands and the inner divines are really two different things. And life offers us many opportunities in teaching us how to listen to what is needed. For most of us it takes many false starts, twists and turns, as we learn to tune into our own knowing.

We cannot be equally devoted to two realities. Either we are inwardly focused and leaning into what is true, or we are outwardly focused and being drawn this way and that way according to other people's dictates—to illusions and untruths. At some point, we must decide which direction and path we want to take. In the end, it becomes about following your own heart, which leads to the opening up and guiding of a higher intelligence.

I acknowledge this isn't always easy to do, and sometimes the stakes are very high. We might be risking a lot by following inner prompting. It can be especially scary and difficult in the beginning, as we learn how to attune to what may be very silent and subtle knowing. Any resistance to listening may make things less clear. As we learn how to listen, it takes practice, self-mastery, and the willingness to make mistakes along the way. Following the still, small voice over time makes that voice more and more obvious until it is eventually second nature—just like a baby learning to crawl, then walk, and then run (to the extent that he is no longer consciously aware of how he is doing it).

It takes courage to be one's natural self, and the world longs for authenticity. Even if it is a trigger for others, even if they turn away and experience shame and embarrassment for witnessing something naked, it is a gift we offer up when we shine like the sun, or cry like the rain.

During my awakening, I would often ask myself, "What is it that I am avoiding? What is it that I am not totally telling myself about what is true?"

What about you? What are you not fully feeling into? What are you not feeling to its core?

You need to stop running from yourself; finally and completely stop, turn around, and face what is creating the gap between what you know to be true and living it

Through programming since childhood, we live in a state of limitation. However, most people find comfort in the familiar, comfort in their parents' belief systems, and comfort in following what society dictates—even if it means going against their internal guidance system.

We create these stories throughout our lives, these narratives that we come to believe, and which truly dictates our lives. We live with so many different personas, and masks. We live an illusion and we believe these illusions. Justifying the most untruthful things within our mind space. And we wonder why our external reality reflects such limitation, such shortfalls and negativity.

This path of healing and awakening is not for the faint hearted, but rather for the one who is ready to commit to it fully. This road of un-becoming will destroy everything you have ever come to believe about the world and about yourself. Towards the end of this journey there will be nothing left but you. You will be more of yourself than you ever were.

Are you willing? You must be willing to give up everything to truly be aligned with the truth of your soul. Your commitment to this path cannot be taken lightly. I find a lot of people embark on this path only to turn back, unwilling to continue, because they fear it is the path of destruction and annihilation. The paradox? It is. However, the destruction is a necessary process to untether one's soul, to lift the veil of illusion, so one can truly step into one's innate power and true essence.

For me this was a complete process of surrender. I had a tendency because of fear, to always try and control everything, so as to ensure a good outcome. I was afraid to be hurt, I was afraid I was not good enough, I was afraid I would never be happy. And this path forced me to surrender all of that. To take my hands completely off the wheel and actually just trust. I had to take many long hard looks in the mirror and truly face the truth and truly face myself. Every part of myself in its rawest form.

The process entailed in this book is a process I have mastered. It is a process that has helped me remove blocks, traumas, and subconscious beliefs quite quickly. It has helped me open and access my gifts and abilities, and it has allowed me to be connected, ever so deeply, to the Divine. It is the most wonderful thing to live on purpose to experience unconditional love. For unconditional love is what we are.

Imagine doing the internal work and actually seeing real, exciting, and beautiful shifts in your external life. As I began to heal, I experienced amazing and wonderful abundances and opportunities. I began to truly trust in the universe, trust in myself, and overcame all my fears of the future.

The below is a channelling I received just before I completed writing this book:

And as you begin to know that the pale that you are in, is breaking, and as it breaks to only realize that there is another pale just below this pale. Know that you will always be guided. You have lots of great wisdom within you and the more you look the more you remember, so keep looking and keep seeing that wow I do have all of the answers within Me. We also want you to know that you are surrounded by many many angels, giving you lots of insight, so please just quiet your mind and hear it now, as right now you reap the energies of remembrance, with grand and amazing new ideas. You are about to make a huge breakthrough here that will be the first of your kind.

CHAPTER 10:

And I Say to You...

Nothing to hold onto anymore

When one gets to a later stage during the spiritual awakening journey, we get to a point of completely transcending and integrating self or ego (separate sense of self), integrating all aspects dark and light. And towards the end of this stage, it feels as if nothing can save you, it feels like you have completely failed, being stripped away of all your beliefs, opinions, stories, personas and identities.

Nothing to hold onto anymore. It could feel as if you have failed miserably. Experiencing the Great Spiritual Death.

But this feeling of failing, of death - is an important step, because it allows the persona or belief that one needs to succeed – in order to get somewhere – to completely die off. The Ego cannot grasp onto ideas, concepts or tangibles anymore, in order to keep this illusion of success and failure alive. When this persona or belief dies, we come to realize that this whole failure and success thing is really just an illusion, and something we have come to believe.

When you realize you need to apply the spiritual principles to your life, and you fear-based mind gets triggered, it's tempting to run away. Sometimes your old life will seem more comfortable and appealing.

You may want to run away from your feelings because they ask you to step up. There will be tons of reasons to hide.

Running away is the easiest and the least satisfying road to travel. Anything that you try to hide from will eventually find you. Thus, keep your heart wide open to anything that surfaces in your life. You'll meet your soul there.

During the spiritual awakening process, it's essential to find the pace that suits you and be flexible. If you don't see the changes that you wished for yet then perhaps it's not the right timing, or you haven't learned some lesson. But there are never concrete walls in front of you, keep moving and creating your path.

Imagine getting to a point where being someone, something, a failure or success didn't mean a thing, didn't define who we are. That we are already powerful beings, inherent with divine love and are the creators of our reality. Imagine getting to the absolute realization that we are more than just the constructs of our mind, our stories, our beliefs and our attachment to it.

Imagine coming to the absolute realization of who this really is that is standing in your shoes and looking through your eyes.

A good friend of mine once quoted a line from a poem by Oriah Mountain Dreamer called "The Invitation." The quote was: "It doesn't interest me if the story you are telling me is true. I want to know if you can disappoint another to be true to yourself; if you can bear the accusation of betrayal and not betray your own soul." That says it all!

The journey of awakening and enlightenment brings about the realization of truth: first through great doubt, then through great surrender, then through great spiritual death, and ultimately through embodiment and expression of this realization.

So, starting right now, in this moment, I am asking you to become Source-God. I am asking you to take your stand, to stand undeniably steadfast in your intention to awaken to the truth of you. The power of this simple, immovable, and intentional stand to be liberated in this lifetime can propel you to awaken to the simple fact that you and all mankind are liberated, pure beings and awakeness itself. Period.

At every moment from here on out, have the intention to directly experience truth: your true liberated self.

Don't think about the truth or what it could be. Rather, directly return to your experience here, now, moment to moment.

Be present. Be love. Be the creator.

And I say to you: Go forth dear ones, go be living examples of the Divine which you are.

Unveil the illusions, delusions, projections, and perceptions and completely Un-become. This, in and of itself, is liberating. It will allow you to be a true vessel of divine love and divine grace.

And so, I pose the question once again:

Do you now know who and what you are?

Do you feel that inherent knowing, remembrance, and that slight vibration within your being now?

Imagine being a dolphin, thrown into a bowl with goldfish... and realizing you were free all along.

I love you...

About The Author

Riana Arendse (Seraph Erakiel) is an international bestselling author, and world-renowned Sage for The Highest Order of Angels - The Seraphim. A Globally-Celebrated Visionary Spiritual Teacher whose Teachings through her Work, Wisdom, Live Events and Media Interviews have already helped countless people throughout the world find Inner Peace, Healing and Greater Fulfilment in their lives. In Riana's experience, it was the gift of her own suffering which allowed her to have a much greater and grander viewpoint, cultivating an unparalleled level of Spiritual Mastery that has drastically changed both what she teaches and the way she teaches. It is one's suffering and one's darkest moments according to Riana that becomes the greatest catalyst for authentic awakening, enlightenment and healing. Riana's Core Teachings remind us that We Are Creator experiencing itself through energy and form, only to realize and experience itself once again as Creator. In conjunction with creating a movement of positive world change, Riana Arendse founded THE SERAPHIM ORDER FOUNDATION, a non-profit initiative that enables ideas, goals, and ventures that are aimed at awakening the Sovereign Divinity of all Mankind.

RANA'S WEBSITE: https://www.rianaarendse.com/

RIANA'S FACEBOOK PAGE: https://www.facebook.com/rianaarendse...

INSTAGRAM: https://www.instagram.com/rianaarendseofficial/

222

Printed in Great Britain
by Amazon

32566580R10130